Sports, Fitness, and Motor Activities for Children with Disabilities

Sports, Fitness, and Motor Activities for Children with Disabilities

A Comprehensive Resource Guide for Parents and Educators

Edited by
Rocco A. Aiello

ROWMAN & LITTLEFIELD
Lanham • Boulder • New York • London

Published by Rowman & Littlefield
A wholly owned subsidary of The Rowman & Littlefield Publishing Group, Inc.
4501 Forbes Boulevard, Suite 200, Lanham, Maryland 20706
www.rowman.com

Unit A, Whitacre Mews, 26-34 Stannary Street, London SE11 4AB

British Library Cataloguing in Publication Data

Library of Congress Cataloging-in-Publication Data

Names: Aiello, Rocco, editor of compilation.
Title: Sports, fitness, and motor activities for children with disabilities : a comprehensive
  resource guide for parents and educators / edited by Rocco Aiello.
Description: Lanham : Rowman & Littlefield, [2016] | Includes bibliographical
  references and index.
Identifiers: LCCN 2015038597 | ISBN 9781475818178 (cloth : alk. paper) |
  ISBN 9781475818185 (pbk. : alk. paper) | ISBN 9781475818192 (electronic)
Subjects: LCSH: Sports for children with disabilities—Handbooks, manuals, etc. |
  Physical education for children with disabilities—Handbooks, manuals, etc.
Classification: LCC GV709.3 .S68 2016 | DDC 796.087—dc23 LC record available at
  http://lccn.loc.gov/2015038597

♾™ The paper used in this publication meets the minimum requirements of American
National Standard for Information Sciences—Permanence of Paper for Printed Library
Materials, ANSI/NISO Z39.48-1992.

Printed in the United States of America

I would like to dedicate this book to my wife, Jill, for standing alongside me throughout my career in education and writing this book. I wouldn't have come this far to increase my knowledge and move my career forwards if it wasn't for your outstanding support, encouragement, and unwavering love over the past twenty years. Thank you for being a positive influence in my life.

Contents

Foreword

Physical activity for individuals with disabilities has been advocated for several decades.

Today, the value of physical activity and sport for individuals with disabilities of all ages is increasingly recognized. Efforts to increase opportunities for physical activity and sport are particularly enhanced in the United States via its constitution, federal and state legislation, and accepted educational value. Clearly, schools and communities have a key role and responsibility in providing experiences in these areas. However, many barriers exist to inhibit optimal offering and participation.

In society, although many individuals and groups advocate and provide desirable services, there remain barriers to services that need to be overcome. It is not unusual that when this occurs, it is the "people" that have to "make things happen." In the case of physical activity and sport in schools and communities, the family (particularly the parents and guardians) has a critical role and responsibility for enhancing opportunities for youngsters with disabilities.

This book has been designed to help fulfill this role and responsibility. It does this by providing information regarding a developmental perspective for participation, offering an analysis and specific examples regarding the role and responsibilities of parents/guardians in assisting school and community experiences. This book offers examples of specific physical activity and sport experiences (inclusive and disability specific experiences); explaining the processes that are important for collaborating between school, district, and community entities; presenting ways of modifying sport experiences; and offering instructional strategies for increased participation in school and community programs.

A key part of the book is a description of situations in which parents have worked to involve their children in a variety of physical activity and sport opportunities. These examples demonstrate how the efforts of parents and guardians pay off.

It is important to point out that the book editor and chapter authors are successful teachers and leaders in the field of adapted physical education and sport. They work with children and their parents and guardians seeking optimal services. They believe in the importance of writing a book related to the roles and responsibilities of parents/guardians so that youngsters can benefit from these services. They hope and believe their contributions in this book will help to offer very important services to youngsters with disabilities.

Joseph P. Winnick, Ed.D.
Distinguished Service Professor Emeritus
Kinesiology, Sport Studies, and Physical Education
The College of Brockport, State University of New York
Editor of *Adapted Physical Education and Sport*

Acknowledgments

A book is never the sole effort of the author. Actually, this book is the results of several professional educators and colleagues in the area of Adapted Physical Education.

I would like to express my sincere gratitude to each chapter authors for their dedication in co-authoring this book and for their tireless efforts in promoting increased physical activity for all individuals regardless of age, or ability level. This book has truly been a team effort.

Chapter 2, Dr. Cathy Houstin-Wilson
Chapter 3, Dr. Justin Hagleman and Mr. Mathew Marcell
Chapter 4, Dr. Lauren Lieberman and Amaury Samalot-Rivera,
Chapter 5, Dr. Ronald Davis and Dr. Garth Tymeson and
Chapter 6, Dr. Ellen Kowalski and Linda Webbert

I will forever be grateful to my former college professor, Dr. Joseph Winnick. Dr. Winnick has been instrumental in providing me guidance and word of wisdom throughout my undergraduate and graduate school career. It is truly an honor that Dr. Joseph Winnick wrote the Foreword for this book.

All of the students with and without disabilities that I have had the pleasure to teach in St. Mary's County Public School in Maryland and at the New York State School for the Blind.

I would like to express my sincere appreciation to the Greer Family: Mandy, Jim, Alyssa, and James for allowing me to take their picture for the front cover of the book.

I am also indebted to Susan Lassiter for her words of wisdom and encouragement in writing this book.

From book proposal to final completion, I'm indebted to Christine Fahey, assistant editor for Education, and Sarah Jubar, acquisitions editor for Rowman & Littlefield, for their talent, support, and attention to detail in bringing this book to life. You both were a joy to work with on this project.

Chapter 1

Increased Physical Activity for Children with Disabilities

Rocco Aiello

"In order for man to succeed in life, God provided him with two means, education and physical activity. Not separately, one for the soul and the other for the body, but for the two together. With these means, man can attain perfection."

—Plato

Timothy was diagnosed with Autism Spectrum Disorder at the age of two years. Timothy is now six and attends the local elementary school, where he is included in the general education and physical education classes.

Timothy's physical education class meets three times every two weeks for 35 minutes per class. In addition to his general physical education (GPE) class, Timothy receives an additional 30 minutes per week in adapted physical education (APE). In total, Timothy receives 83 minutes per week of physical education, far less than the recommended 150 minutes established by the National Association of Sports and Physical Education (NASPE).

Prior to receiving adapted physical education, Timothy was given a formal assessment by his APE teacher, Mr. Brown, using the Test of Gross Motor Development-2 (TGMD-2). On the basis of the TGMD-2 findings, Mr. Brown developed two goals, with two objectives per goal, for Timothy to work on during the school year in both his general and adapted physical education classes.

At the end of the school year, Mr. Brown was invited to Timothy's annual review to discuss his Individual Education Plan (IEP) progress report. Unfortunately, on looking at the data collected by Mr. Brown, discovered that Timothy had fallen short of meeting his set goals and objectives. He now lags behind his age-appropriate peers by two years.

Timothy's parents voice their concerns regarding the lack of progress made on Timothy's goals for APE. Both parents request additional time in APE for Timothy so that he can work toward his IEP fitness and motor skill goals. Unfortunately, due to Timothy's schedule during the day, and Mr. Brown being an itinerant APE teacher traveling to other schools in the district, the IEP team is unable to recommend additional time and service for Timothy in APE.

Mr. Brown has recommended that Timothy participate in community recreation and leisure programs that facilitate fitness and motor skill development, in addition to his general and APE classes. Mr. Brown will assist Timothy's parents as they pursue a variety of inclusive after-school programs offered in the community.

PHYSICAL EDUCATION IN PUBLIC SCHOOLS

In today's educational environment, the amount of time students receive in physical education has rapidly decreased, making way for an increased number of academic programs. In order for public schools to save money, a greater emphasis is placed on meeting federal mandates on improving academic test scores and, unfortunately, less funding and time goes toward physical education programs.

The Surgeon General recommends that youth receive at least 60 minutes of moderate physical activity every day, which includes muscle strengthening and cardiovascular endurance activities (U.S. Department of Health and Human Services, 2008). Needless to say, our school-aged children might not be receiving the recommended 60 minutes per day of physical activity.

In 2001, the federal government passed the No Child Left Behind Act (NCLBA), which was set to improve standardized test scores of American children. The NCLBA mandates that all children meet the required national level in reading, math, and other basic skills. However, the law did not mention the importance of health or physical education for students in education.

According to the Institute of Medicine (2003), nearly fifty percent of school administrators have reported cutting significant time from GPE classes and recess to devote more time to reading and mathematics in the classroom ever since the NCLBA was passed. Reducing the amount of time in physical education and recess in response to the requirements of the NCLBA, schools could be depriving their students of essential elements they need in order to perform better in the classroom.

For children with disabilities, this can be detrimental, as these children have fewer opportunities to develop fitness and motor–skills along with increased social interaction among peers. Children with disabilities greatly benefit from having a balance in all aspects of their lives, including cognitive (thinking), affective (emotion/feeling), and psychomotor (physical/kinesthetic) development.

The three domains of learning—cognitive, affective, and psychomotor development—belong to Bloom's Taxonomy of Learning. This is the cornerstone by which physical education teachers develop their curriculum that consists of skill development, participation, and collaboration between all students.

The most effective physical education curriculums are those that incorporate all three domains. Nevertheless, having a limited amount of time in physical education reduces the likelihood that children with disabilities will not be as successful in the areas of fitness, motor ability, intellectual skills, character development, and personal social-emotional adjustment among others (Pangrazi, 1991). The benefits of physical education are universal for all children, including those with disabilities.

Physical education provides increased physical activity that helps control weight, builds lean muscles, reduces fat, and contributes to a healthy functional cardiovascular system, hormonal regulatory system, and immune system. It also promotes strong bones, muscles and joint development, and decreases the risk of obesity (CDC, 2011).

Recent reports indicate that only 3.8 percent of elementary schools, 7.9 percent of middle schools, and 2.1 percent of high schools offered students daily physical education or its equivalent for the entire school year (Lee, Bergerson, Fulton, & Spain, 2007). The President's Council on Fitness, Sports and Nutrition reported that physical activity is 4.5 times lower for children and youth with disabilities compared to their peers without disabilities (U.S. Department of Health and Human Services, 1996).

This is not encouraging news for children with disabilities, as it makes it less likely for these children to receive the time, energy, and encouragement to maximize their fitness and motor skill potential. Physically fit children are less likely to miss school, partake in risky behaviors, get pregnant; overall they will improve academically, which are all associated with better outcomes in school (Taras, 2005).

For more than 100 years, the NASPE, currently known as SHAPE America, has provided guidance and leadership to physical educators. In a position statement developed by NASPE, it emphasizes that elementary students should receive daily quality physical education for a minimum of 150 minutes per week and 225 minutes per week devoted to middle and high school students (NASPE, 2009).

NASPE established this guideline in order for school-aged children to receive the appropriate amount of time necessary to develop skills related to cognitive, affective, and psychomotor development. Physical education is an important discipline that is unique to educating all children, which contributes to all three domains along with cooperative learning and differentiation of instruction.

The goal that NASPE established is for educators to emphasize the value of developmentally and instructionally appropriate programs in physical education. Bearing this goal in mind, physical educators should train all children to enable them to possess the knowledge, skills and confidence to become and remain physically active for a lifetime.

PHYSICAL EDUCATION AND ACADEMIC PERFORMANCE

In 2010, the U.S. Department of Health and Human Services, Center of Disease Control (CDC) and Prevention, reported on the increased body of research that strongly supports the collaboration between school-based physical activities, including physical academic performance among school-aged children. The results suggest that physical education and increased physical activity may help advance academic performance for many students and is not likely to hinder academic progress.

The CDC further implies that physical activity can have a positive impact on cognitive skills, positive attitudes, and academic behavior, all of which are important components of improved academic performance. It fact, physical education helps all children, especially children with disabilities, to cope with stress and anxiety. It helps build self-esteem and a positive self-image of their bodies and physical skills. With increased self-esteem comes improved academic performance, which results in more self-confidence.

It is a known fact that exercise directly impacts behavior and brain development. Offering all children the opportunity for daily quality physical education can improve fitness and motor skill development and strengthen their brainpower. This suggests that a healthier child is more likely to become a better learner.

Nevertheless, children have very little opportunity for increased physical education time during the school day due to prolonged periods of academic classes. This contributes to a loss of attention and concentration, which can directly impact a child's academic performance.

AFTER-SCHOOL EXTRACURRICULAR ACTIVITIES

An advantageous direction in which parents, educators, and community leaders can overcome the marginalization of physical education for their children is to take advantage of extracurricular activities in their community.

The CDC reported that adults with disabilities are three times more likely to have heart disease, a stroke, diabetes, or cancer than those without disabilities (May, 2014). Current research has indicated that nearly fifty percent of adults with disabilities receive no aerobic or physical activity. Community recreation and leisure programs are a critical element in the quality of life for all individuals, including those with developmental and physical disabilities.

According to the 2008 Physical Activity Guidelines for Americans, strong evidence correlates that children and adolescents benefit from physical activity resulting in improved cardiorespiratory and muscular fitness, bone health, cardiovascular and metabolic health biomarkers, and favorable body composition. This is especially important for individuals with disabilities.

Community inclusive recreation and leisure programs can be a welcome addition for increased physical activity for individuals with disabilities. With support and input from parents, teachers, advocates of inclusion, and recreational professionals, increased opportunity for participation in community programs can be both a goal and a process (Ray, 2002).

Parents with children with disabilities have always known the importance and value of integrated activities in school and community programs. Children with disabilities and their parents are encouraged to actively seek out accessible and *inclusive* physical activities in their communities.

All children, especially children with disabilities, are at a pivotal point in education when it comes to schools reducing the time allocated for increased physical activity during their physical education class and recess time. However, parents and educators can seek out other options in their community by looking into recreational programs and fitness centers that offer increased physical activity for their children beyond the school day.

TECHNOLOGY AND PHYSICAL ACTIVITY

In the past few decades technological advances used in educational teaching—such as incorporating iPads, video games, and interactive smart boards—have made major impact in the school system. Technology used in today's educational curriculum is designed to help keep students engaged and improve their learning experience.

The continuous pace with which technology is growing is shaping the way teachers engage their students and broaden their knowledge base. It also allows teachers to explore other alternatives that help students to enhance their learning techniques in many ways.

In physical education, technology has steadily evolved with the use of pedometers, accelerometers, heart rate monitors, and interactive sport and movement video games making it easier for students to be involved in movement activities. For children with disabilities the use of assistive technology is clearly defined in the Individuals with Disabilities Education Act (IDEA) of 2004 (Public Law 108–446), which identifies assistive technology devices as

> any item, piece of equipment or product system, whether acquired commercially off the shelf, modified, or customized, that is used to increase, maintain, or improve the functional capabilities of children with disabilities.

For children with disabilities, assistive technology, like pedometers and video games, can be a great educational tool for increased motor performance, socialization, along with tracking students' performance and monitoring their progress.

For example, Johnny, a student diagnosed with Duchenne's Muscular Dystrophy, is entering high school as a freshman and is required to take physical education class. Johnny's parents are adamant that he be included with his age-appropriate peers in the GPE class. However, due to Johnny's limited mobility, the adapted physical educator recommends Johnny utilize the Xbox 360, a piece of assistive technology in GPE.

The Xbox 360 allows Johnny to manipulate a joystick with minimal hand/wrist movement, allowing him to interact with a variety of sports games offered. What makes this assistive technology so special is that Johnny is able to play a variety of sports games with other classmates, thus providing increased social interaction.

Playing a sports game like football, golf, hockey, or baseball allows Johnny to participate in a way he would not be able to do with most real-world sports. Johnny is very enthusiastic about participating in physical education and is making new friends while playing with Xbox 360. Johnny's mom also notices an increase in his excitement and eagerness to participate in physical education class. Johnny's parents decided to purchase the Xbox 360 for home use so that Johnny can continue to play sports games and be able to invite friends over as well.

Johnny's parents noted that without the use of assistive technology in physical education, their son might not be able to earn the required physical education credit needed for graduation. Johnny's mom was resolute about not having Johnny simply sit on the sidelines and "observe" and earn his physical education credit in that capacity. Utilizing video sports game technology allowed Johnny to actually *participate* in some form of motor movement while having increased social interaction with other students.

Technology is transforming how we perceive and partake in physical activity for all students, especially students with disabilities. The use of assistive technology has a positive effect on having all students engaged in increased physical activity and socialization, which, in turn, stimulates them physically and mentally.

In physical education it is important to look for alternative ways to integrate technology into physical education (P.E.) classes that supports educational strategies and keeps children engaged in physical activity and learning (Juniu, 2011). Perhaps the use of technology can help encourage students to be more physically active and help positively change exercise behaviors in a way that students will take it upon themselves to be more physically active.

For parents of children with disabilities, there are many ways to integrate assistive technology into the home or community that incorporates movement activities and sports video games. It is important to understand that assistive technology is an alternative resource that can enhance learning and movement potentials for all children.

The use of technology has become an integral part of the home environment, and that is most prevalent among the youth population (NASPE, 2009). However, it does not replace responsible teaching, it merely adds to the increased physical activity, socialization among friends and family, and a greater appreciation of the benefits of physical activity.

SUMMARY

Today's educational curriculum in the public schools has marginalized physical education programs, making them a low priority. Ironically, physical education is being overlooked at a time when the nation cannot afford to do so. Additionally, with the onset of technology (i.e., iPads, iPhones, and computer games), children continue to engage in sedentary lifestyle behaviors that are associated with multiple risk factors for negative health-related outcomes.

Again, it is without question that children benefit from physical activity, and children with disabilities are no exception. In addition to, a child's school physical education program, children should have the opportunity for increased participation in after-school recreation, sports, and fitness programs which promotes physical, emotional, and social well-being among all children. When children with disabilities are provided with an opportunity to take part in increased physical activity, they develop new friendships by increased interactions and communication among other peers (Aiello, 2014).

Parents are the first and most important advocate and role model for their child's development. Coordinating between the school and community can be a critical element in optimizing the motor and physical fitness skills that are needed for children with disabilities. Achieving increased physical activity by participating in school and recreational programs is the key to their success.

These programs allow children to relieve stress, maximize their energy level, enhance their social skills, and increase their physical activity, and therefore avoiding the possibility of childhood obesity.

Parents and family members who take an active role in their child's educational growth help to promote a positive difference when it comes to behavior, academic performance, and increased participation in school. This also includes voluntary involvement in extracurricular physical activities and sports.

This book has two purposes: (1) to provide parents and others who work with children with disabilities information about the importance of participating in after-school sports and physical activity programs and to help them understand that children with disabilities have a greater chance to engage with their nondisabled peers in ways often not possible during the school day and (2) to share information regarding the laws that impact schools and after-school programs for children with disabilities.

The book places emphasis on parents as advocates for their child's rights when it comes to participating in school and community recreation and leisure programs. Each chapter has vignettes addressing real-life situations involving children with disabilities that offer greater insight into the chapter's objectives and settings.

The book provides useful information on utilizing a variety of instructional strategies when teaching children with disability. These instructional strategies can be beneficial to a child with a disability when developing the necessary skills to be successful in a variety of sports and recreational settings.

Finally, Appendix A offers a wide variety of Adapted Sports Organizations that can be located throughout the United States along with valuable resources specific to the disability population. Appendix B highlights general modifications for a variety of disabilities such as: autism, behavior disorders, communication and understanding, limited mobility and gross motor skills (such as cerebral palsy, spina bifida and muscular dystrophy), and hearing and visual impairments.

REFERENCES

Aiello, R. (2014). Adapted Physical Education: Students with disabilities often want to participate in physical education and sports, and schools have an obligation to make that happen. *Principal Leadership* 4(8), 18–19.

Center for Disease Control and Prevention [CDC] (2011). Physical activity & health. Retrieved from: http://www.cdc.gov/physicalactivity/everyone/health/index.html#.

Center for Disease Control and Prevention [CDC] (2014). Adults with Disabilities: Physical activity is for everybody. Retrieved from: http://www.cdc.gov/vitalsigns/disabilities/.

Individuals with Disabilities Education Act of 2004 (IDEA) (PL 108-446), 20 U.S.C 1400 (2004). Retrieved from: http://idea.ed.gov/download/statute.html.

Institute of Medicine (2013). Educating the Student Body Taking Physical Activity and Physical Education to School. Retrieved from: http://www.iom.edu/Reports/2013/Educating-the-Student-Body-Taking-Physical-Activity-and-Physical-Education-to-School/Report-Brief052313.aspx.

Juniu S. (2011). Pedagogical uses of technology in physical education. *Journal of Health, Physical Education Recreation and Dance (JOPERD)*, 82(9), 41–49.

Lee, S. M., Burgeston, C. R., Fulton, J. E., & Spain, C. G. (2007). Physical education and physical activity: Results from the school health policies and programs study 2007. *Journal of School Health*, 77(8), 435–463

NASPE (2011). National Association for Sport and Physical Education. Physical education is critical to educating the whole child. (Position Statement). Reston, VA: Author. Retrieved from: http://www.shapeamerica.org/.

National Center on Health, Physical Activity, and Disability: Physical Activity, Leisure and Recreation for Youth with Disabilities: A Primer for Parents. Retrieved from: http://www.ncpad.org.

Pangrazi R. P., & Dars P. W. (1991). *Dynamic physical education for secondary school students: Curriculum and instruction*. New York: Macmillan; Toronto: Collier Macmillan Canada.

Ray. T. (2002). Principles for Adapting Activities in Recreation Programs and Settings. Retrieved from: http://www.nchpad.org/108/837/Principles~for~Adapting~Activities~in~Recreation~Programs~and~Settings.

Taras H. (1995). Physical activity and student performance at school. *Journal of School Health*, 75(6), 214–218.

U.S. Department of Health and Human Services, Centers for Disease Control and Prevention (2006). The President's Council on Physical Fitness and Sports. Retrieved from: http://health.gov/PAguidelines/.

U.S. Department of Health and Human Services (2008). 2008 Physical activity guidelines for Americans: Be active, healthy and happy. Retrieved from: http://health.gov/PAguidelines/.

U.S. Department of Health and Human Services Centers for Disease Control and Prevention (2010). The association between school-based physical activity, including physical Education, and Academic Performance. Retrieved from: http://health.gov/PAguidelines/.

Chapter 2

Early Childhood Development

Cathy Houston-Wilson

Molly and Jack Parker were excited to welcome their child Marcus into the world. Marcus was a beautiful baby who brought a lot of joy to his parents. As Marcus grew, it became evident that he was not able to accomplish tasks that other children seemed to do so easily. Concerned, his parents brought him to their pediatrician, who recommended that Marcus receive a neurological evaluation.

The neurologist determined that Marcus had a central nervous system disorder and connected the Parkers with their local Early Intervention agency. The Parkers were overwhelmed by both the diagnosis of their child's disability and the number of professionals who now appeared in their lives.

The Early Intervention agency assigned the Parkers a service coordinator who helped arrange the various assessments needed to determine appropriate services as well as services that the Parkers needed to better provide for their son. Over time, the Parkers learned more about early intervention and the services they were entitled to. They also learned how to interact with and encourage Marcus to become an active learner by engaging him in daily motor activities to enhance his overall development.

The purpose of this chapter is to provide information on early childhood development and the benefit of physical activity to enhance the overall development of young children. Special attention is also devoted to children with special needs.

GROWTH AND DEVELOPMENT

Early childhood is the period of time from birth until five years, which includes infants, toddlers, and preschoolers. These young children grow

11

and develop at a rapid rate and parents and caregivers should provide ample opportunities to foster their development. The three areas of development consist of cognitive (understanding), social and emotional, and physical development. Although there are three specific areas of development, they are not developed in isolation of one another.

Each time a child engages in an activity, all three areas of development can be enhanced. For example, when a baby reaches for a rattle and shakes it, she is enhancing her motor skills. When the rattle makes noise because of the shaking, she is learning about cause and effect (if I shake the rattle, it makes noise), which enhances cognitive development. And when the parent or caregiver smiles and reacts positively to the behavior, the child is experiencing positive social interaction which enhances social-emotional development.

It is clear from this example that the primary way in which young children learn and develop is through movement. It is also obvious that you do not teach young children in the same way you would teach older children and adolescents. They simply do not have the capacity to sit in a chair and be lectured to. They must experience the world around them by acting physically upon it. And there is no need to try and separate development, as all movement enhances the overall development of the child.

Since young children cannot decide what toys to buy or what activities to participate in, parents and caregivers must provide children with ample toys to play with, free space to move around in, and numerous opportunities for interaction with others. One important concept to consider when determining types of toys to supply or activities to engage in is known as developmental appropriateness.

DEVELOPMENTALLY APPROPRIATE PRACTICE

For an item or activity to be deemed developmentally appropriate, parents and caregivers should consider the age of the child and the child's ability level. Children who experience disabilities, delays, or who may be at risk for delays may need additional support from parents and caregivers to achieve the same or similar goals as those of typically developing children.

Regardless of ability level, all children benefit from developmentally appropriate movement programs. Often, well-meaning parents and caregivers want to encourage their child to be active and play games like the rest of the family; however, it would be considered developmentally inappropriate to give a toddler a standard-sized basketball and expect the child to shoot at a driveway basketball hoop. The ball is too big and heavy for his small hands and the hoop is too high for any success to occur.

Rather a small playground ball and laundry baskets scattered around the area would encourage the child to play with the ball and "shoot it" into the laundry baskets. As the child "makes a basket" and parents cheer, the child experiences positive social interaction and learns the purpose of the activity.

Further, physical skills are being developed as the child runs around, bounces a ball, and tosses it into a basket. Everything about this activity is appropriate because it takes into consideration the age of the child and the child's ability level. Further it ensures success. Not only do young children need to have interactions with the world around them; they must also be able to successfully act upon it. These successful experiences help children to develop a positive self-concept and shape their self-esteem and self-worth.

In addition to enhancing development, movement and physical activity have other benefits. For example, having young children engage in successful motor activities early on and throughout their lives significantly reduces the likelihood that they will struggle with obesity and other health-related issues as adults. They will be more likely to try new activities and have a greater likelihood of participating in physical activity later in life as adults (Sanders, 2002).

MOTOR DEVELOPMENT

Based on the information described above, it is clear that young children need to be afforded opportunities to engage in physical activities to enhance their development. What may not be clear, however, is the type of motor activities that are best suited to meet the developmental needs of the child.

Motor development follows a sequential process, and there are approximate ages and stages that define motor development (Gallahue, Ozmun, & Goodway, 2011). It is important to note here that although children will follow a sequential pattern of development, the rate at which this development occurs can vary greatly. Some children may be able to walk independently by eight months, while others, especially those with delays or disabilities, may not achieve this milestone until they are a year or older.

The progressive nature of development can be illustrated in the following examples. An infant must be able to sit up independently before she can pull to stand. A toddler needs to be able to walk before she can gallop, and a preschooler needs to be able to bounce a ball before she can dribble it. The first part of each of these examples demonstrates that certain tasks must be mastered before a child can attain higher levels of functioning.

There are four stages of movement that consists of reflexive, rudimentary, fundamental, and specialized movement (Gallahue, Ozmun, & Goodway, 2011). Reflexive movements are involuntary and occur during the first year of life. As reflexes subside or become inhibited, rudimentary movement takes hold. Reflexive movement generally becomes inhibited by age one. However, children with certain forms of disability affecting the central nervous system may have delayed reflexive inhibition or a reflex may never subside. These children will require movement programs that adapt to their needs and may require proper positioning to engage in physical activities.

Rudimentary movement, on the other hand, is the first form of voluntary movement and lays the groundwork for future motor skill development. Rudimentary movement is considered a building block for more advanced fundamental movement patterns. Similarly, fundamental movement patterns serve as the building block for specialized movements, which are seen in sport-related activities.

The following section more fully describes the two main areas of motor development that are evident in early childhood development—rudimentary and fundamental movements. Included are examples of how parents and care-givers can facilitate the acquisition of these motor skills, which, as described above, helps to develop the whole child. While all children can benefit from the experiences discussed below, it is crucial for parents and caregivers of young children with delays or disabilities to create and assist them as needed to experience the benefits of these activities.

Rudimentary Movement

The first form of voluntary movement, known as rudimentary movement, occurs in a predictable sequential manner and covers the age range from birth to approximately two years (Gallahue, Ozmun, & Goodway, 2011). Children with disabilities or delays may continue in this phase longer than usual, but through appropriate intervention of deliberate activities, gains will be realized.

One of the first voluntary movements an infant needs to master is control of the head and neck, which allows the child to see and take in the world around her. Next comes the control of the trunk, which allows the child to move into a sitting upright position unassisted. Once a child can sit independently, she can then try standing upright, first by holding onto something, for example, parents' hands or a tabletop, and then unassisted.

Once the child has mastered these basic skills, she is ready for horizontal movements such as scooting, crawling, creeping, and walking on all fours. Not every child will perform horizontal movements in the same way, but some variation of these movements will be seen prior to gaining the ability to walk upright.

Generally, a child will need assistance during his first few attempts at walking upright and may fall several times while learning this newfound skill.

As long as the area is clear from objects, a few falls here and there should not cause great concern. There are a multitude of toys on the market that are geared toward assisting a child to learn how to walk upright, for example, push toys. These toys have wheels that keep the speed at which they move in check. They are inviting in color and purpose.

For example, a toy lawn mower is one kind of a popular push-toy. When a child pretends that she is mowing the lawn, she is essentially gaining control of the upright walking position. Other forms of rudimentary movement that are mastered early in development are the ability to reach, grasp, and release.

Some may wonder why every time a child grasps an object she either holds on to it very tightly or drops it. The reason is that she is gaining motor control over the process of releasing. Initially it is difficult to release an object and so the child's grip appears very tight. As development occurs and the child is able to release the object, she may find this new action exciting and want to repeat it over and over again.

Gaining control over these fine motor skills is essential to later independence when the child can hold a spoon and feed himself. Again, some children with developmental delays may experience difficulty with these milestones, so parents and caregivers need to bring items to the child and when necessary provide physical assistance to facilitate the acquisition of these motor skills.

Fundamental Movement Skills

Fundamental movements are the next phase of development that young children will experience. Fundamental movement is broken down into three components: balance, locomotor movements, and manipulative movements (Gallahue, Ozmun, & Goodway, 2011).

There are two forms of balance: static balance, or balance that is stationary, and dynamic balance, or moving balance. Examples of static balance include pulling to a standing position and maintaining that upright position unassisted or standing on one foot. Dynamic balance is the ability to maintain an upright position while walking in a straight line or maintaining equilibrium when moving the body through space such as when the child does a forward or backward roll.

Many children with developmental delays or disabilities may have difficulty with balance, which can minimize their effectiveness at other forms of fundamental movement at a later stage. Providing children with a variety of tasks to encourage balance is highly recommended. Drawing lines on the sidewalk with chalk and asking the child to walk along the line or placing pillows on the floor to practice rolling are all appropriate activities to enhance balance.

Locomotor movements include the ability to walk, run, jump, hop, gallop, slide, and skip. Each of these skills helps to shape the development of the next. For example, the child needs to master the ability to walk before she can run.

Running requires a brief period where both feet are off the ground, which is a precursor to jumping. Jumping requires the ability of the child to take off and land on two feet, while the hop requires the child to take off and land on one foot. Hopping is followed by the ability to gallop, which is essentially a combination of a walk and a leap in a forward motion, while this same combination can be seen in a sideward motion known as a slide.

Skipping is the most advanced form of locomotor movements and is a combination of a step and a hop done sequentially alternating feet. Children need to have many opportunities to attempt these skills and should be given cues and feedback on performance to help facilitate mature movement patterns. Some children with delays or disabilities may need physical assistance in order to perform these skills correctly, and providing appropriate levels of support promotes success and the willingness to continue to try new activities without fear of failure.

Manipulative skills are any skills that use implements for the action. Examples of manipulative skills include throwing, catching, kicking, and striking. The most important factor to consider when providing young children with the opportunity to engage in manipulative activities is to be cognizant of developmentally appropriate practices as described above.

Equipment that is provided to young children must take into consideration their age, stature, and ability level. Equipment should be sized appropriately, light enough to manipulate, and soft enough so it does not present a hazard, and there should be enough items available so the child does not have to search for the object which may, in turn, cause the child to lose interest.

PARENTS AND CAREGIVERS AS FACILITATORS

The unique thing about working with young children to enhance their development is that the primary role adults take in the process is that of a facilitator. As discussed previously, young children are not miniature adults and do not learn the same way as older children and adolescents do. Everything they learn is learned through the experiences they engage in. Therefore the role of the parent or caregiver is to facilitate the interaction of the child within their environment (Sanders, 2002). The best way to do this is to create environments that are safe and inviting.

Environmental arrangement is the key to facilitation. There should be child-sized toys and options to encourage different forms of play, which would result in self-initiated repetition. This means that the child finds pleasure in the activity and repeats it over and over again. Through this process the movement becomes more refined and can easily be expanded so the child is willing to try new activities.

Adults are instrumental in creating challenges for the child, but should not dictate how the child should play with a particular item, unless safety is a concern. Allowing children to direct their play is a concept known as child-directed play and is a highly recommended early childhood teaching strategy.

GUIDELINES FOR ACTIVE MOVEMENT

Professionals in early childhood education have established recommended guidelines for active movement for infants, toddlers, and preschoolers (SHAPE America, 2009). These guidelines are reviewed below. Parents and caregivers should take an active role in ensuring their child comes as close to meeting these guidelines as possible.

It is recommended that infants interact with their parents or caregivers in activities that promote the exploration of their environment throughout the day. In addition, the environment should not restrict movement for long periods of time; for example, placing a child in a playpen or car seat for extended periods of time is not recommended, nor is it appropriate.

Parents and caregivers need to provide ample opportunities for infants to practice their newly developed skills. Placing toys within reach of the child will encourage the child to sit upright and play and placing toys slightly out of reach will encourage horizontal movements to attain the object.

For an infant to be on their stomach, known as tummy time, is also highly recommended. Since the American Academy of Pediatrics (2012) recommends that infants be placed on their back to sleep, infants have little time to strengthen their back and neck muscles unless they are deliberately placed on their stomach. However, during this time, parents and caregivers need to supervise the child to be sure that nothing constricts the child's airway. Inviting equipment that is colorful, easy to manipulate, and varied in size and texture are also ideal to promote motor skill interactions.

It is further recommended that toddlers accumulate at least 30 minutes of daily structured physical activity and 60 minutes or more of daily, unstructured physical activity throughout the day (SHAPE America, 2009). Additionally, they should not be sedentary for more than 60 minutes at a time except when sleeping. As discussed previously, during this phase of development, toddlers are moving from rudimentary movements to fundamental movements, and providing them with free space and appropriate equipment will greatly enhance their development.

Finally, in terms of preschoolers, it is recommended that they should accumulate 60 minutes of daily structured and 60 minutes to several hours per day of daily unstructured physical activity. Additionally, they should not be sedentary for more than 60 minutes at a time except when sleeping.

GUIDELINES FOR CHILDREN WITH SPECIAL NEEDS

Infants, toddlers, and preschoolers with special needs are afforded special services known as early intervention to help overcome or minimize the effect of delay or disability in one or more of the following developmental areas: cognitive, physical, communication, social-emotional, and/or adaptive development (Houston-Wilson, 2011).

Infants and toddlers are provided early intervention services through local governmental agencies. These agencies are required to assess the child and create a plan that supports both the child and the family. This plan is known as an Individualized Family Service Plan (IFSP). The plan will identify the services the child is eligible for and the person responsible for providing the service. The services the child receives may be conducted in the home, at an early intervention facility, or at a day care center, whatever best meets the needs of the family.

All intervention programs are provided at no cost to the family. Preschoolers with delays or disabilities are serviced through school districts and are protected under the guidelines of a federal law known as the Individuals with Disabilities Education Act (2004). As required for infants and toddlers, preschoolers must also be assessed to determine their special needs and an appropriate plan of action must be established. This plan, known as an Individualized Education Plan (IEP), identifies all the services and service providers that will be afforded to the child.

Child-specific goals and objectives are also identified on the plan. School districts may create early intervention preschool classes within the district or provide the service in the home or at center-based facilities (Houston-Wilson, 2011).

Understanding your rights and responsibilities as a parent of a child with a delay or disability will allow you to become an advocate in securing appropriate services for your child, which in turn will help your child reach his or her full potential.

SUMMARY

Parents and caregivers are in the best position to provide opportunities to assist in the growth and development of their child. Recommended strategies include following developmentally appropriate best practices. These practices call for providing ample time, appropriate equipment, and environmental arrangements to facilitate movement.

In addition, parents and caregivers should take the role of a facilitator and follow the child's lead during play. Some children, however, due to delays or disabilities will need physical assistance to engage in and complete tasks. Having an understanding of typical growth and development as summarized above positions parents and caregivers to enhance the overall development of their child.

REFERENCES

American Academy of Pediatrics. (2012). *A Parents' Guide to Safe Sleep.* Elk Grove Village, IL: Author.

Gallahue, D.L., Ozmun, J.C. & Goodway, J. (2011). *Understanding Motor Development: Infants, Children, Adolescents, Adults.* Boston: McGraw-Hill.

Houston-Wilson, C. (2011). Infants and toddlers. In J.P. Winnick (ed). *Adapted Physical Education and Sport.* Champaign, IL: Human Kinetics.

Individuals with Disabilities Education Improvement Act of 2004 (IDEA). 20 USC 1400.

Sanders, S. (2002). *Active for Life: Developmentally Appropriate Movement Programs for Young Children.* Champaign, IL: Human Kinetics.

SHAPE America. (2009). *Active Start: A Statement of Physical Activity Guidelines for Children from Birth to Age Five* (2nd ed.). Reston, VA: Author.

Chapter 3

Parents/Guardians Role and Responsibilities

Justin A. Haegele and Matthew Mescall

Cody and Rebecca Foster have been happily married for fifteen years and live in a small suburban town outside of a large metropolitan area. Growing up, both were very active in sports and physical activity. Cody played varsity tennis in high school and many different intramural and pick-up sports during college. Rebecca was a competitive rugby player throughout her high school and college experiences, and still plays sporadically with a local club team.

The Fosters have two children: Jenna and Jessica. Jenna is in sixth grade and is very active in sports and physical activities during and outside of school. She is a starting outfielder on the middle school softball team and one of the captains of the track and field team. When she is not practicing with varsity sports teams, she is participating in other physical activities with her friends at the park. Jenna has dreams of one day being a college athlete like her mother.

Jessica, Cody and Rebecca's other daughter, is far less active than everyone else in the family. Jessica is in third grade and does not participate in any sports during the school day or during after-school hours. When Jessica was younger, she was very active during physical education and would always happily play at the park. However, while Jessica would like to participate in some sports or activities now, she does not believe there are any opportunities for her to do so.

Jessica has partial vision loss caused by juvenile macular degeneration. Macular degeneration is a progressive visual impairment that affects one's central vision, sensitivity to light, and causes difficulty distinguishing small details like recognizing faces. Since her vision began to worsen, Jessica and her parents have seen her opportunities to be physically active diminish.

Her school's physical education teacher is unsure of how to accommodate her needs in class, where she regularly sits out rather than participating.

Further, her school refuses to allow her to participate in after-school programs because of fear of further injury. Rebecca and Cody also struggle to find community-based programs that are willing to take Jessica as a student. At this point, this physically active family is at the brink of giving up on their youngest daughter leading a physically active and healthy lifestyle.

INTRODUCTION

The favorable and life-enhancing impact of regular physical activity participation on the overall health of individuals has been well documented. According to the Centers for Disease Control and Prevention (CDC, 2011), regular engagement in physical activity can lead to decreases in health-related issues such as obesity, diabetes, hypertension, anxiety, depression, and heart disease.

Individuals who develop a physically active lifestyle at an early age can decrease the chances of developing these health-related issues throughout childhood as well as later in life (Sothern, Loftin, Suskind, Udal, & Blecker, 1999).

However, the previously described scenario of the Foster family is far more common than one might think. School-aged individuals with disabilities, like Jessica, tend to be less physically active than their typically developing peers (Kim, Conners, Hart, Kang, & Kang, 2013; Pan, Frey, Bar-Or, & Longmuir, 2005).

National data indicates that approximately twice as many individuals with disabilities report being inactive than those without disabilities (Rimmer, 2008). This lack of physical activity participation can lead to several major health issues throughout the lifespan. For example, national surveys demonstrate that 37 percent of individuals with disabilities report having poor health status, in comparison to only 8 percent of those without disabilities (Rimmer, 2008).

Obesity is one such health concern that has become a national agenda due to its high prevalence. Studies indicate that school-aged individuals with various disabilities tend to have higher obesity rates than those without disabilities (e.g., Curtin, Answerson, Must, & Bandini, 2010; Lieberman & McHugh, 2001; Sohler, Lubetkin, Levy, Soghomonian, & Rimmerman, 2009).

Fortunately, research suggests that school-aged individuals with disabilities who regularly participate in physical activity can decrease the chances of developing health-related issues, such as childhood obesity (Rimmer, Rowland, & Yamaki, 2007). However, children with disabilities will likely not participate in physical activities unless parents are actively involved in seeking these opportunities (Arnhold, Young, & Lakowski, 2013). Therefore, the purpose of this chapter is to provide parents and guardians, like the

Fosters, with essential information about their roles and responsibilities in influencing physical education, physical activity, and recreational opportunities for their children with disabilities.

Specifically, this chapter will discuss (a) the advocate role of parents, including a review of the legal rights of children with disabilities; (b) what information parents can communicate to physical education teachers; and (c) tips parents can use to promote physical activity for their child. This chapter intends to provide information for parents that they can utilize to access, enhance, and promote physical activity–related opportunities for their children.

PARENTS ROLES AS ADVOCATES

Parents of children with disabilities report many barriers that may hinder the ability of their child to participate in physical education and community-based recreation and sport programs. Some such barriers include a (a) lack of communication between parents and educators/ community programmers, (b) lack of knowledge or training of the physical education teacher/ community programmers, (c) fear of the teacher/programmer or parent in regard to safety, and (d) lack of appropriate programs (An & Hodge, 2013; Moran & Block, 2010; Moran, Taliaferro, & Pate, 2014; Perkins, Columna, Lieberman, & Bailey, 2013).

In order to overcome these and other barriers to physical activity participation, parents must feel empowered to actively advocate for their children's needs and desires. Two keys for parent advocacy include parental involvement and active and reciprocal communication (Dimmock & O'Donoghue, 1996; Perkins et al., 2013).

Parental Involvement

Parental involvement is a critical feature to overcoming barriers and making improvements in the achievement and performance of children with disabilities in physical activity contexts (Dimmock & O'Donoghue, 1996). Parental involvement can take on several forms and can fit different lifestyles. For example, parental involvement can include acting as support personnel during activities that include their child, participation within the organization that provides those activities, or volunteering as an assistant coach on a sport team (An & Hodge, 2013).

Regular parental involvement allows parents to have a sound understanding of the activities that their children are participating in because of their close proximity and experience with those activities. Active involvement may also allow parents to help make decisions about how activities are presented to children, such as including strategies that best fit the learning style of their children. In addition to those examples provided, parental involvement can also take the shape of regular communication with the child's physical educator or community-based programmer.

Active and Reciprocal Communication

A critical ingredient to establishing parental involvement is active and reciprocal communication (An & Hodge, 2013; Perkins et al., 2013). However, parents tend to communicate more regularly with special education teachers or other individuals in schools or community programs rather than with physical education staff. Further, parents tend to wait until yearly meetings (i.e., IEP meetings) for updates on their child. These strategies decrease the ability of physical education teachers and community programmers to directly discuss issues, successes, and failures of students with parents on a regular basis.

Rather than waiting for yearly meetings, or speaking with other teachers about physical activity performance, parents should feel empowered to communicate actively, reciprocally, and often with their physical activity providers. This type of relationship can facilitate conversations about many important elements that will be discussed throughout this chapter.

For example, one such topic may be successes and interests of a child that the educator may see throughout the year. Since physical education teachers incorporate multiple units into their classes throughout the year, they have the ability to gage the student's interest in a number of different activities.

In addition to receiving updates on the performance of the child, regular communication with physical education teachers will allow parents to advocate for their child's and the family's best interests. This topic is further explored in a following section of this chapter, What to Communicate to Physical Education Teachers, which describes several critical pieces of information that parents should share with their child's physical education personnel.

Turning Barriers into Hurdles

When parents are empowered to actively advocate for their child, barriers to physical activity tend to fall. While teachers or community programmers may feel as though they have a lack of knowledge when working with children with specific needs (Moran et al., 2014), parents can educate those individuals on the abilities and limitations of their children through active communication.

Parents also tend not to enroll their children in community programs due to fear of injury or ridicule from peers (Moran & Block, 2010). However, an involved parent will have an understanding of what is going on day-to-day within the program and can help modify those activities to their child's needs.

Lastly, parents report that there are fewer opportunities for their children to participate in activities. In many cases though, children with disabilities can participate in community activities or physical education activities with simple modifications. A parent who advocates for their child can make these modification suggestions to teachers or programmers to include their child successfully.

Communicating suggestions can be especially important when children are young and in a developmental level of learning. Youth sports at the developmental level should emphasize the development of a variety of different skills specific to that sport (see figure 3.1).

Parents should remind coaches and other parents that this is what youth sport is all about, not winning or losing. In scenarios like these, parents can continue to be involved by actively supporting their child. For example, a parent may go out on the field with their child to encourage them or provide them with support or safety. These accommodations are easily made when parents, coaches, and officials communicate these needs beforehand and agree on how this can be done.

When advocating for a child with a disability, an important tool for parents to have is a full understanding of the federal laws and mandates that influence their child's education and opportunities in the community. These documents provide supportive materials for parents when discussing and requesting physical activity–related services and opportunities for their child. Several important laws and mandates that influence those opportunities are discussed throughout this text in other chapters.

Developmental Youth Sports should Emphasize............	
Physical Skills	Motor Skill Learning
Socialization Skills	Exploration
The Ability to Play as a Team Member	Fitness Level
Fair Play	Manipulative Skill Learning
Self-esteem	Confidence
FUN!!	

Figure 3.1

WHAT TO COMMUNICATE TO PHYSICAL EDUCATION TEACHERS

As mentioned previously, active and reciprocal communication between parents and physical education teachers is an essential component to promoting physical activity and motor development opportunities for children with disabilities. Physical education teachers are the individuals within the school system who have the most direct influence on a child's physical activity. These individuals can act as advocates within the school walls to ensure that children with disabilities are getting the experiences that they need.

When physical education teachers choose activities for classes, they typically take several variables into considerations, such as the developmental and age appropriateness of activities. Developmental appropriateness refers to choosing activities that allow each student to participate and be successful (Hodge et al., 2012), whereas age appropriateness takes into consideration activities that the student's peers without disabilities of a similar age would be participating in (Haegele, 2014). In addition to these considerations, physical education teachers may also consider several important pieces of information that can be communicated by parents.

One such example of important information that can be communicated by parents is the personal goals that they may have for their child. For example, a parent may want their child to complete a 5k run or learning how to weight train. These goals can be expressed to the physical education teacher and become incorporated into the physical education curriculum for that child.

Some additional topics that should be discussed with physical education staff include

- family physical activity preferences
- activities that are available outside of school
- modifications that are best for a specific child
- each child's preferred reinforcer
- content that can be taught in class to influence physical activity at home

Family Physical Activity Participation

One of the most important topics a parent can discuss with their physical education teacher is the physical activities that the family participates in outside of school. This can include the favorite activities of the parents, a sport played by siblings, or activities that everyone does together.

When a parent discusses what physical activities a family participates in together during their leisure time, physical education teachers can then include those activities in their instruction throughout the school day (Hodge, et al., 2012). The physical education teacher can tailor their instruction specifically toward the physical activity preferences of the children, which will complement the family's extracurricular activity. An educator can also find and use adapted equipment that allows for the child to be most independent and successful during those activities.

Communicating physical activity preferences to the physical education teacher not only benefits the student, but also the growth and togetherness of the family. Unfortunately, many families stop participating in physical activities together because they believe that their child with a disability is unable to be included (Hodge et al., 2012).

Practicing these skills during school hours can contribute to families bonding through physical activity again. For example, if Rebecca and Cody Foster communicate that Jenna's sister is an active softball player, their physical education teacher can work on several softball-related skills with her during physical education (e.g., fielding a groundball and playing beep baseball). After improving these skills in class, Jenna and Jessica can then participate in physical activities and bond together as siblings outside of school.

Community Activity Availability

A second important topic to discuss with physical education teachers is the physical activities that are available and accessible in the community for each child. While teaching in a specific area, physical education teachers should have a clear understanding of the community-based options for physical activity that are available to students with and without disabilities.

By understanding the physical activities that are available in a given community, physical education teachers can provide a more meaningful physical activity experience to their students by focusing on activities that students can do outside of school.

However, all activities that are available in a given area may not be available to each and every family. Therefore, parents should communicate which activities within the community are available to them specifically. This is particularly important in very large school districts that include several smaller towns that may offer different physical activity opportunities, or for parents who have limited transportation to facilities.

Again, when a physical education teacher has an understanding of the community physical activity options that are available to families, they can work on skills for those activities in school to enhance the likelihood of students participating in those activities outside of school.

Child-Based Modifications

When physical education teachers plan instruction for children with disabilities, there are many different ways that they modify activities for each child.

For parents to facilitate and promote physical activity participation outside of school, it is important for them to also have an understanding of what modifications work best for their child to ensure success. Therefore, another important topic for parents to discuss with physical education teachers about is equipment/ activity modifications.

But what types of modifications are there? Within each activity, physical education teachers may make modifications to equipment, boundaries, or rules (Haegele & Mescall, 2013). Equipment modifications can include using a larger or softer ball, lowering a basket, or making a goal larger, or deflating a ball to make it slow down (Haegele & Mescall, 2013).

Boundary modifications include changes to the playing area, such as using caution tape to mark off boundaries or increasing or decreasing the size of the playing area. Lastly, rule modifications include changes to gameplay, such as giving offensive players more space between themselves and the defender (Haegele & Mescall, 2013).

In addition to modifying activities, there are additional accommodations that are available to children with disabilities that can help promote physical activity. One such accommodation that is commonly used to help children with disabilities in physical education is personnel support, such as paraprofessionals.

Paraprofessionals work alongside physical educators and are considered a related service for individuals with disabilities who receive service under IDEA (Haegele & Kozub, 2010). Paraprofessionals can provide several types of support that can enhance physical education experiences for those with disabilities. Examples are provided in figure 3.2. Parents who believe that extra personnel support, such as paraprofessionals, would benefit their child should discuss this possibility with their physical education staff and school administrators.

It is important for parents to understand that when teaching activities, physical education teachers have control of activities. This means that physical education teachers can/do modify activities to promote the success of their students (Brian & Haegele, 2013). Again, it is essential for parents to have an understanding of which modifications help their child to be the most successful during physical activities in school to help promote participation outside of school.

Preferred Reinforcers

Another important topic that parents should discuss is each child's preferred reinforcer. A reinforcer is an addition to or subtraction from the environment (e.g., a high five and a sticker) that increases the future likelihood of a child demonstrating a particular behavior (Cooper, Heron, & Heward, 2007). Reinforcers are typically used by parents and the physical education teacher to

Roles of Paraprofessionals in Physical Education
• Assist student's movements as needed.
• Keep students focused, on task, and quiet.
• Repeat instructions when necessary.
• Prompt students for transitions.
• Help children with behavior plans adjust to inclusive settings.
• Provide verbal cues or physical assistance if needed.
• Provide additional modeling (physical, tactile, visual).
• Work one-on-one if necessary.
• Help ensure safety.
• Help facilitate socialization with peers.

Figure 3.2

provide further incentive to students with disabilities to participate in physical activities or complete tasks.

There are several benefits to parents and physical education teachers communicating about reinforcers. First, if parents are familiar with the reinforcers being used in physical education, they can use the same reinforcer at home when participating in physical activity. According to Alber-Morgan (2010), in order for behaviors, such as physical activity, to be emitted regularly in settings outside of school, students must contact similar or the same reinforcement in those settings as well. By using the same reinforcers, parents can support and build upon the work that is already being done at schools.

A second benefit is that parents can educate physical education teachers about the preferences of each child. Since each child has different interests, the physical education teacher may attempt to use reinforcers that are generic (e.g., a high five) prior to more individualized (e.g., a sticker of a favorite sports team) reinforcer.

When parents communicate preferences to teachers, they make it easier for teachers to use more specific reinforcers that are tailored to each individual child, therefore strengthening the reinforcement. Overall, this reciprocal communication between parents and physical education teachers about reinforcers can promote increased physical activity participation for children with disabilities inside and outside of school.

Content to Promote Home-Based Physical Activity

In addition to the previously discussed topics, parents can also request that physical education teachers instruct specific content within their classes that can promote physical activity participation at home. Two such types of content that are becoming increasingly popular in physical activity classes that can promote outside of school physical activity are (a) self-management skills and (b) physical activity homework.

Self-management Skills

Self-management skills refer to the personal application of strategies that produce a desired change in behavior (Cooper et al., 2007). These types of skills are important because they ensure that students function with the greatest degree of independence possible. Self-management skills include setting goals and monitoring those goals, and can be used in many different types of skills or activities.

Physical activity journals are one type of activity that physical education teachers can introduce to students which promote self-management skills (Ballinger & Deeny, 2006). Physical activity journals ask students to develop goals and record information about their physical activity participation, such as the activities they participated in, with whom, and for how long, each day. Parents can work with their children to help them record their physical activity participation each evening before they go to bed.

A second activity that can contribute to self-management skills is the use of physical activity monitors, such as pedometers. Pedometers are objective, cost-effective measures of physical activity that count the total number of steps taken (Albright & Jerome, 2011). Different types of pedometers have been validated for a number of different disabilities, including the use of talking pedometers for individuals with visual impairments (Haegele & Porretta, 2015), like Jessica. Again, the use of pedometers can promote physical activity participation outside of school by using self-management skills.

Physical Activity Homework

Lastly, parents can request that physical education teachers assign physical activity homework to their children. Assigning physical activity homework ensures that students with disabilities are using the skills that are being covered during physical education outside of school. It is important that physical activity homework reflect what students are doing in school and that physical educators assign only those activities that students have already mastered during the school day (Mitchell, Barton, & Stanne, 2000).

Physical education homework can include both structured and unstructured physical activity participation (Smith & Claxton, 2003). Some examples can include asking students to (a) repeat activities completed in physical education, (b) participate in an activity with a family member for a specific amount of time, or (c) researching an activity to perform in the community.

Some other suggestions for physical activity homework include (a) asking the physical education teacher to include the parents in the homework assignments as much as possible and (b) ensuring that students are held accountable for completing homework assignments in class (Smith & Claxton, 2003).

TIPS TO PROMOTE PHYSICAL ACTIVITY FOR YOUR CHILD

Thus far, this chapter has discussed several elements to help parents advocate for physical activity experiences for children with disabilities. The purpose of this section is to describe several tips parents can use themselves to promote physical activity participation for their children. These tips can be used in isolation, or in combination with one another. Parents should be encouraged to discuss these tips, as well as the successes and failures of these strategies, with their child's physical education teacher or other physical activity service providers.

Protection v. Overprotection

It is understandable that parents want to ensure their child's safety, including when they are participating in physical activities. This can include protecting a child's physical safety (i.e., will my child get injured when participating in sports) and emotional safety (i.e., will my child fail and get embarrassed when attempting to complete tasks). However, it is possible for parents to protect their child to a degree where they are unable to experience activities that typically developing children experience throughout the lifespan. This type of behavior can be referred to as overprotection.

Overprotection can have several undesirable repercussions for children with disabilities. For example, overprotection can influence children to be more apprehensive while participating in activities, which can increase the likelihood of getting injured. Second, children whose parents are overprotective may choose to participate in more sedentary activities rather than physical activities. A higher rate of sedentary activities can contribute to unhealthy weight gain and likelihood of health-related issues. Third, overprotection may thwart a child's ability to interact fittingly with the environment or their peers.

Rather than being overly conscious about the safety of a child because they have a disability, parents should be encouraged to maintain the same level of support (and fear) during activities that they would have for any children.

Everyone falls. Everyone gets hurt. In many ways, falling is a learning tool during physical activities that allows our bodies to teach us something about what we did. Parents of children with disabilities tend to see many benefits of physical activity participation, but "overprotection" is one such behavior that may decrease the quality of their children's experiences.

Promote 60 Minutes of Activity of Day

The Society of Health and Physical Educators (SHAPE, 2014) encourage all school-aged individuals to participate in 60 minutes of daily physical activity for health-related outcomes. However, those minutes may not all be available during school hours. Therefore, parents should help promote and facilitate active movement and physical activity at least 60 minutes a day.

For a child with a disability, some of that activity time should be spent on meaningful activity to help develop skills, strength, stamina, body and self-awareness, and/or range of motion. Many of the following activities can be done as a family or can include neighborhood friends to help promote socialization. Some such activities include

- Having a catch
- Active video gaming
- Shooting hoops
- Yoga
- Going to a playground
- Going on a hike or walk
- Biking or roller-skating
- Playing disc golf
- Tag games outside
- Following a fitness routine
- Going bowling
- Ice skating
- Swimming

Like having a peer mentor in school, parents might want to reach out to a trusted neighborhood friend to help act as a mentor or activity buddy to help promote activity and socialization.

Parents as Physical Activity Role Models

Previous sections discussed the important role that activity selection and participation of families play in influencing physical activity opportunities for children with disabilities. In addition to participating in activities as a family, family members can help educate children with disabilities about physical activities by acting as role models. As a child watches or listens to their parent participate in or speak about a physical activity, they learn about and form opinions on those activities.

If parents or guardians are active, display valuing physical activity, and make physical activity an essential part of their lives, their child with a disability can also assume that physical activity is an essential part of their lives and follow suit. Since school-aged individuals are encouraged to participate in 60 minutes of physical activity daily for health-related concerns (SHAPE, 2014), parents should also consider participating in an hour of activity to demonstrate the value of participation.

This does not mean that children with disabilities must participate in the same exact activities or at the same level of intensity as parents. Rather, children can gain an understanding of the value of activity by observing their family demonstrate that same value. Again, opportunities to gain an understanding of the value of physical activity should be offered to the child in the same way as anyone else. Therefore, accomplishments and successes of all family members should be celebrated and rewarded to demonstrate the value of physical activity participation and success.

In addition to acting as a role model in regard to participating in physical activity, parents can also play act as a role model while teaching their children about sports from the perspective of a spectator. Sports and physical activity play such an important role in our culture. Many families spend time together watching major sporting events each year (i.e., the Super Bowl). This time acts as a bonding experience for many children with their families.

However, children with disabilities may not pick up on learning a sport by watching it on television or listening to sport talk radio like their age appropriate peers who are typically developing. Therefore, parents should take the opportunity to model language and behavior when watching sporting events with their family.

There are several benefits of learning about being a sport spectator for children with disabilities. In addition to building further opportunities for family bonding, this type of modeling can help facilitate language and social skills while also increasing self-esteem and confidence when children are interacting with other youth who are interested in sports. For example, as the Super Bowl approaches, Jessica Foster typically hears many of her peers discuss the game. However, she may not have a keen understanding of the nuances of football, and doesn't understand a lot of the terminology of the sport. If her parents take time to model and teach the language and behaviors of being a spectator at sports such as football, there is a higher likelihood of her participating in these social interactions.

Seek out Community Programs for Children with Disabilities

Another strategy parents can use to facilitate physical activity participation is to enroll their children in community-based programs. Community recreational programs can provide excellent physical activity opportunities for all individuals, including those with disabilities.

Two types of community physical activity programs that are becoming increasingly common are inclusive programs and specialized sport programs. Inclusive programs are those that include children with disabilities at a natural proportion with peers without disabilities on the same sports teams or in the same activities. These activities typically focus on both physical activity skills and socialization skills.

Specialized sport programs are those that are specifically designed for individuals with disabilities. These are becoming increasingly common, particularly in cities and large suburban areas. For example, the Little League Baseball Challenger (LLBC) division provides baseball experiences that are designed specifically for individuals with disabilities.

LLBC division programs are available in different locations throughout the country and their website (www.littleleague.org) provides information on grant programs to foster development of more local programs (Porretta, 2011).

Inclusive and specialized sport programs typically have modifications and accommodations built into the program that ensure the success of their participants. The individuals who tend to coordinate and coach programs of this nature are either other parents of children with disabilities or adapted physical education teachers from a local school district.

To find programs like these, parents should (a) search the internet of the local area to see what is available, (b) speak with other parents in the area about physical activity opportunities, or (c) contact their child's adapted physical education teacher about local opportunities to be active outside of school.

Use Adapted Equipment at Home

Another idea to help motivate your child to be physically active is to buy or build modified equipment as a gift during the holidays or for a birthday. Having adapted equipment at home allows students to use that equipment during activities with their friends and family and during community sport programs.

When children receive sport equipment as a gift, they tend to value the equipment and associate it with the special someone who gave it to them. Further, if the gift is received at a family or friend gathering, it also allows the child to see his/her family and friends enthusiastic reactions to the thoughtful gift, allowing the child to accept it more easily even though it may be different from a "typical" piece of equipment. It can also encourage families to find creative ways to use the equipment with the child.

Parents should feel encouraged to discuss what equipment to purchase for their child with their physical educator.

Investigate After-school/Community Programs

As previously discussed, places where children with disabilities can gain valuable physical activity experiences can include after-school and community programs. However, not all programs are appropriate for every child. Parents should be encouraged to investigate after-school and community programs prior to enrolling their child. Typically, these programs are open and welcoming when parents want to do their homework about a program, and parents should simply call ahead of time and schedule an appointment with the facility.

When investigating after-school and community programs, most parents want to ensure that programs are providing a safe, nurturing recreational curriculum where children with disabilities can have fun and learn through age-appropriate activities that foster physical, social, emotional, and cognitive development. However, many parents do not know all of the questions they need to ask to get these answers. Figure 3.3 provides a checklist that parents can use when investigating programs to ensure that each of these needs are being met.

Listen to the Voice of the Child

A final tip for promoting physical activity opportunities for children with disabilities is for parents to listen to the voice of their child. When promoting physical activity opportunities for children with disabilities, parents tend to expose their child to what they believe would be best for them. However, what is best for a parent, or what the parent believes would be best for the child, may not always be the child's preference.

One such example of when this occurs is when parents decide between enrolling their child in inclusive programs or specialized sport programs. As discussed previously, inclusive programs are activities that individuals with disabilities participate in with age-matched peers without disabilities.

In most cases, the perceived benefit of programs like these is the social interactions between those with and without disabilities (Block & Obrusnikova, 2007). However, research demonstrates that not all children with disabilities find inclusive environments to provide or promote positive social interactions

Program Evaluation Checklist		
Name of Organization _____		
Locati _____ Date _____ on _____		
Contact _____ Phone _____ Person		
Program Questions:	Yes	No
• Does the program philosophy match the parents' philosophy?		
• Does my child find this sport or physical activity interesting?		
• Does the level of play (i.e., competitive, recreational) match the needs of the child?		
• Does my child have the physical capability to participate in this program?		
• Will the program provide the support needed for the child?		
• Does the program provide activities that promote social interactions?		
• By participating in this program, will my child increase their physical health?		
• By participating in this program, will my child improve their social skills?		
• By participating in this program, will my child improve their independence?		
• By participating in this program, will my child improve their motor skills?		
• By participating in this program, will my child improve their confidence?		
• Can parents be involved (i.e., coach, assistant)? If so, how?		
Staff Questions	Yes	No
• Does the staff have training for working with children with disabilities?		
• Does the staff have experience working with children with disabilities?		
• Does the staff have child abuse and bully prevention training?		
• Can parents visit and observe while the program is in session (after joining)?		
• Will the program staff take time to communicate with the parents?		
Logistical Questions	Yes	No
• Is the program within a reasonable distance to home/ work/ school?		
• Is the program insured?		
• Does the program provide transportation for students? If so, what is the cost?		
• Is there a cost for the program? If so, how much?		

Figure 3.3

(Fitzgerald, 2005; Goodwin & Watkinson, 2000; Healy, Msetfi, & Gallagher, 2013). Conversely, children with disabilities can experience social isolation (Fitzgerald, 2005) or bullying (Dane-Staples, Lieberman, Ratcliff, & Rounds, 2013) in these types of settings.

The purpose here is not to turn parents away from inclusive physical activity environments, as many children with disabilities also have positive and meaningful experiences when participating in sport and physical activity with their peers without disabilities (Goodwin, 2001; Seymour, Reid, & Bloom, 2009). Rather, the purpose is to encourage parents to discuss physical activity choices and opportunities with their child prior to enrolling them in programs. By listening to the voices of children of disabilities, parents and physical activity providers can further individualize activities and opportunities for those children while providing physical activities that are tailored to their interests and needs.

SUMMARY

Physical activity is an essential component to the lives of all individuals, including those with disabilities because of the favorable impact regular participation has on one's health. However, it is unlikely for individuals with disabilities to be engaged in physical activities and sport unless parents are actively involved.

This chapter described the role and responsibilities of parents and guardians in promoting physical activity, physical education, and recreational opportunities for their children with disabilities. The importance of and critical features of the advocacy role of parents/guardians was discussed, including important information parents can use when advocating for their child's best interests. Descriptions of important information to communicate with physical education teachers were provided.

Lastly, the chapter concluded with several tips that parents can use to enhance physical activity participation and opportunities for their children with disabilities. It was the objective of the authors of this chapter to provide meaningful and timely information that parents, like Cody and Rebecca Foster, can use to further enhance physical activity opportunities for their children in order to contribute to a happy and healthy lifestyle.

REFERENCES

Alber-Morgan, S.R. (2010). *Using RTI to teach literacy to diverse learners, K-8.* Thousand Oaks, CA: Sage Publishing.

Albright, C., & Jerome, G. (2011). The accuracy of talking pedometers when used during free-living: A comparison of four devices. *Journal of Visual Impairment and Blindness, 105*(5), 299–304.

An, J., & Hodge, S.R. (2013). Exploring the meaning of parental involvement in physical education for students with developmental disabilities. *Adapted Physical Activity Quarterly, 30*(2), 147–163.

Block, M.E. & Obrusnikova, I. (2007). Inclusion in physical education: A review of literature from 1995–2005. *Adapted Physical Activity Quarterly, 24*(2), 103–124.

Brian, A., & Haegele, J.A. (2014). Including students with visual impairments: softball. *Journal of Physical Education, Recreation, and Dance, 85*(3), 39–45. doi:10.1080/07303084.2014.875808.

Center for Disease Control and Prevention [CDC] (2011). *Physical Activity & Health.* Retrieved from http://www.cdc.gov/physicalactivity/everyone/health/index.html#.

Cooper, J.O., Heron, T.E., & Heward, W.L. (2007). *Applied behavior analysis* (2nd ed.). Upper Saddle River, NJ: Pearson Education, Inc.

Curtin, C.M., Anderson, S.E., Must, A., & Bandini, L. (2010). The prevalence of obesity in children with autism: A secondary data analysis using nationally representative data from the National Survey of Children's Health. *BMC Pediatrics, 10*(11), 11. doi: 10.1186/1471-2431-10-11.

Dane-Staples, E., Lieberman, L., Ratcliff, J., & Rounds, K. (2013). Bullying experiences of individuals with visual impairments. The mitigating role of sport participation. *Journal of Sport Behavior, 36*(4), 365–386.

Davis, R., Oliver, A., & Piletic, C. (2007). The paraeducato's roles and responsibilities in physical education. In L.J. Lieberman (Ed.), *Paraeducators in Physical Education* (pp. 15–23). Champaign, IL: Human Kinetics.

Dimmock, C.A.J., & O'Donoghue, T.A. (1996). Parental involvement in schooling: An emerging research agenda. *Compare: A Journal of Comparative and International Education, 26*, 5–20. doi: 10.1080/0305792960260102.

Fitzgerald, H. (2005). Still feeling like a spare piece of luggage' Embodied experiences of (dis)ability in PE and school sport. *Physical Education and Sport Pedagogy, 10*(1), 41–59. doi:10.1080/1740898042000334908.

Goodwin, D.L. (2001). The meaning of help in PE: Perceptions of students with physical disabilities. *Adapted Physical Activity Quarterly, 18*(3), 189–303.

Goodwin, D.L. & Watkinson, E.J. (2000). Inclusive PE from the perspective of students with physical disabilities. *Adapted Physical Activity Quarterly, 17*(2), 144–160.

Haegele, J.A. (November 2014). Physical activity for youth and adolescents with visual impairments. Webinar available through the American Foundation for the Blind. Retrieved from: http://afb.org.

Haegele, J.A., & Kozub, F.M. (2010). A continuum of paraeducator support for utilization in adapted physical education. *Teaching Exceptional Children Plus, 6*(5), Article 2. Retrieved from: http://escholarshop.bc.edu/education/tecplus/vol6/iss5/art2.

Haegele, J.A. & Mescall, M. (2013). Inclusive physical education. *Division of Visual Impairment Quarterly, 58*(3), 7–16.

Haegele, J.A. & Porretta, D.L. (2015). Validation of a talking pedometer for adolescents with visual impairments in free-living settings. *Journal of Visual Impairment & Blindness, 109*(3), 219–223.

Healy, S., Msetfi, R., & Gallagher, S. (2013). 'Happy and a bit nervous': The experiences of children with autism in PE. *British Journal of Learning Disabilities, 41*(3), 222–228. doi:10.111/bld.12053.

Hodge, S., Lieberman, L., & Murata, N. (2012). *Essentials of Teaching Adapted Physical Education.* Scottsdale, AZ: Holcomb Hathaway.

Kim, T., Conners, R.T., Hart, P.D., Kang, Y., & Kang, M. (2013). Association of physical activity and body mass index with metabolic syndrome among US adolescents with disabilities. *Disability and Health Journal, 6*(3), 235–259.

Lieberman, L.J. & McHugh, E. (2001). Health-related fitness of children who are visually impaired. *Journal of Visual Impairment & Blindness, 95*(5), 272–287.

Mitchell, M., Barton, G.V., & Stanne, K. (2000). The role of homework in helping students master physical education goals. *Journal of Physical Education, Recreation, & Dance, 71*(5), 30–34.

Moran, T.E. & Block, M.E. (2010). Barriers to participation of children with disabilities in youth sports. *Teaching Exceptional Children Plus, 6*(3), Article 5. Retrieved from: http://files.eric.ed.gov/fulltext/EJ879597.pdf

Moran, T.E., Taliaferro, A.R., & Pate, J.R. (2014). Confronting physical activity programming barriers for people with disabilities: The empowerment model. *Quest, 66*(4), 396–408. doi:10.1080/00336297.2014.948687

Pan, C., Frey, G., Bar-Or, O., & Longmuir, P. (2005). Concordance of physical activity among parents and youth with physical disabilities. *Journal of Developmental and Physical Disabilities, 17*(4), 395–407. doi: 1.1007/s10882–005-6622–7.

Perkins, K., Columna, L., Lieberman, L., & Bailey, J. (2013). Parents' perceptions of physical activity for their children with visual impairments. *Journal of Visual Impairment & Blindness, 107*(2), 131–142.

Porretta, D.L. (2011). Team sports. In J.P. Winnick (Ed.). *Adapted Physical Education and Sport* (5th ed.), (pp. 503–527). Champaign, IL: Human Kinetics.

Rimmer, J.H. (2008). Promoting inclusive physical activity communities for people with disabilities. *President's Council on Physical Fitness & Sports, 9*(2), 1–8.

Rimmer, J.H., Rowland, J.L., & Yamaki, K. (2007). Obesity and secondary conditions in adolescents with disabilities: Addressing the needs of an underserved population. *Journal of Adolescent Health, 41*(3), 224–229.

Seymour, H., Reid, G., & Bloom, G.A. (2009). Friendship in inclusive PE. *Adapted Physical Activity Quarterly, 26*(3), 201–219.

Smith, M.A. & Claxton, D.B. (2003). Using active homework in physical education. *Journal of Physical Education, Recreation, & Dance, 74*(5), 28–32.

Society of Health and Physical Educators. (2014). *National standards & grade level outcomes for K-12 physical education.* Champaign, IL: Human Kinetics.

Sohler, N., Lubetkin, E., Levy, J., Soghomonian, C., & Rimmerman, A. (2009). Factors associated with obesity and coronary heart disease in people with intellectual disabilities. *Social Work in Health Care, 48,* 76–89. doi: 10.1080/009873808 2451160.

Sothern, M.S., Loftin, M., Suskind, R.M., Udall, J.N., & Blecker, U. (1999). The health benefits of physical activity in children and adolescents: Implications for chronic disease prevention. *European Journal of Pediatrics, 158*(4), 271–274.

Winnick, J.P. (2011). Introduction to adapted physical education. In J.P. Winnick, *Adapted Physical Education and Sport* (5th ed.) (pp. 3–20). Champaign, IL: Human Kinetics.

Chapter 4

Community Programs

Lauren J. Lieberman and Amaury Samalot-Rivera

Juan Carlos was a new student in Manuel Corchado y Juarbe Middle School. When Juan Carlos, a youth with legal blindness and learning disabilities, arrived the first day of school with his parents, the first teacher they saw was Mr. Rivera, the physical education teacher.

"Good morning, I am Mr. Rivera the PE teacher, welcome to Manuel Corchado y Juarbe School, house of the Panthers! Do you participate in any sports?" asked Mr. Rivera.

Juan Carlos's parents answered that he did not participate in any sport-related activity because he is legally blind. Mr. Rivera very respectfully asked why, and the parents said, "Well, there is nothing out there for children with visual impairments; We just don't know what to do."

Finding appropriate sports, recreation, and leisure programs for children with disabilities can be a daunting process and the number of choices currently does not mirror the breadth and range of opportunities afforded to nondisabled children. This is also true for youth and adults with disabilities who want to get involved into community-based programs.

One of the biggest concerns that parents of children with disabilities have reported is that they don't know what to do once their child reaches age twenty-one as their youth are done with school services. Many parents worry about what their youth with disabilities will do to be integrated and be active members of their communities (Warner, Newman, Cameto, Garza, & Levine, 2005).

Also, many parents don't know where to get information about the available programs that their children and youth with disabilities can participate in their communities.

Like Juan Carlos's parents, there are many parents that simply don't know what to do when it comes to involving their children with disabilities in sports or physical activity programs in their communities. Many believe that because their children have a disability there is nothing out there for them. Others try, but there is often not many things available in the community that meet the unique needs of their child.

In many occasions, individuals with disabilities depend on school- and university-based programs to experience participation in recreation or sport-related activities. Unfortunately, research has demonstrated that a high percentage of youth and adolescents with disabilities do not actively participate in after-school programs, intramurals, community-based programs, or social events (US Government Accountability Office, 2010; National Organization in Disability, 2010).

The benefits of participating in sport and recreation activities for people with disabilities are numerous and have been promoted by professionals in the field. Self-perceptions of bonding to school community, positive social behaviors, better school grades and academic achievement, health-related benefits, and significant reductions in problem behaviors are just some of the benefits reported by the literature (Vandell, Reinser, & Pierce, 2007; Durlak, & Weissberg, 2010; Hodge, Lieberman, & Murratta, 2012).

This chapter will explore program considerations for the implementation of sport, recreation, and leisure programs for children with disabilities after school. It will provide parents, teachers, coaches, and any support personnel with guidance on different variables to consider when identifying and planning for transition services of children and youth with disabilities into their communities through sport and recreational activities.

It is important to note that programing for children with disabilities can be in inclusive programs as well as disability specific programs. Participation should be based on ability, not disability.

WHAT CAN PARENTS DO?

Three things that are extremely important will be mentioned several times in this chapter and can be seen in figure 4.1.

First, the need to ensure that the physical education teacher and/or the adapted physical education teacher is involved in the Individual Education Program (IEP) development process.

Secondly, it is also important to ensure that the physical education program for the child includes every unit their peers are learning to ensure self-determination.

Lastly, it is very important to include sport, recreation, and leisure planning during IEP meetings and transition planning.

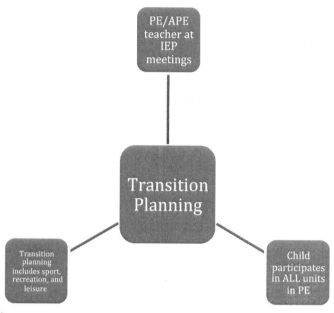

Figure 4.1

Finding the right sport or recreational program for children with disabilities is not necessarily an easy task. Most of the programs available are very specific and in many occasions are university based, which are offered to a limited number of participants. Even with today's access to information through technology, finding the right program will take time and effort. Sometimes, there are programs, but parents simply do not know what to do.

Samalot-Rivera, Aleman & Vega (2015) provided some steps that can be followed when selecting a sport or recreational program for youth with disabilities. Their focus is more related to selecting programs that will promote the child's transition into the community. The steps they provided are the following: (1) see what programs are available in the community, (2) take into consideration the child/youth interests, (3) collaboration between the adapted physical education program and community-based program and parents, and assess youths' progress toward developing transition skills.

Table 4.1 provides more detailed information on each one of these steps.

Table 4.2 provides suggestions for parents for each level of school for their child. The *action plan* is the steps the parents can take and *key players* are the individuals who can help in making each step happen. In some cases the

Table 4.1   Steps to Follow When Selecting Sport or Recreational Program For Youth with Disabilities

1. See what programs are available in the community	A good idea is to connect with your local recreation community department or a YMCA to see what programs they have available. Also see if there are other alternatives that with small modifications will make participation possible. In many occasions, there are University/ College programs available that provide free services to children and youth with disabilities. Make sure to communicate with the physical education or recreation departments of local institutions for the available programs.
2. Take into consideration your child's / youths' interest	Self Determination Theory (Daci & Ryan, 1985) states that when you take into consideration the interests of the student or participant, there are better chances to reach the goals of the program. Literature in special education had demonstrated that when we take into consideration the interests of students with disabilities to determine instruction, there is more likelihood that students will reach their goals. It will also help students to become happier and enjoy what they are doing to increase their self-esteem and chances to succeed.
3. Collaboration between the adapted physical education program and community-based programs and parents	It is important to remember that collaboration is the key to success when dealing with transition from school to the community. Open communication between every person involved in the transition process is necessary. This will increase the opportunities for a more effective transition process to recreation, physical activity and community involvement. It is important to start thinking about transition as early as possible. This will increase chances of success in transition effort made in the future.
4. Assess youth progress for transition skills development	To make sure that learning and progress is taking place, it is imperative to assess youths' progress. Periodic assessment can provide information about areas of improvement and adaptations needed to ensure transition goals are achieved. As mentioned in the previous step, collaboration is the key to success in this process. It is important to identify their progress and the areas that need more support. Consult your adapted physical educators, therapeutic recreationist, or other personnel to make sure this important process takes place.

authors felt there may need to be more information to execute some of these important steps.

The questions below will offer solutions to the issues that may arise with the action plan.

Table 4.2   Action Steps to Take at Different Age Levels Related to Sports and Recreation into the Community

Age level	Action Plan	Key Players
Elementary level	• Ensure the child learns everything his or her peers are learning • Ensure PE is included on the IEP • Communicate periodically with the PE teacher • Start experiencing recreation and leisure offered in the community • Set up play dates with peers in the community • Involve the child in summer programs and camps	• Physical Education/ APE teacher • Special Education Coordinator • Community program coordinators and staff
Middle School	Same action plan as elementary plus: • Ensure the child is an active part of transition goals related to sport and recreation • After-school sport involvement • Make sure PE teacher is part of transition plan meetings • Children should get involved in age-appropriate sports and recreation directed to their functional level	• Physical Education/ APE teacher • Special Education Coordinator • Community program coordinators and staff • Coaches • Athletic Director
High School	Same action plan as above and include the following: • Ensure sport and recreation is included in every IEP and transition meeting along with key players • Ensure goals and objectives related to sports recreation and leisure are included in the transition plan • Start focusing in on preferred sport and recreation • Teach advocacy to overcome barriers to these preferred activities • Ensure there is collaboration between school and the community and ensure that some programming is conducted in the community	• Physical Education/ APE teacher • Special Education Coordinator • Community program coordinators and staff • Coaches • Athletic Director

FREQUENTLY ASKED QUESTIONS

1. Who do you go to for help with structure and professionals involved in the IEP?
   a. PE/APE teacher
   b. Special education teacher

2. Where can parents go for information regarding after-school and summer programs for children with disabilities?
   a. School district, local universities web sites
   b. Local YMCA or private sport or recreational programs
   c. Office of Recreation and Sports
   d. Look at summer programs specific to individuals with disabilities (Camp Abilities, Camp Inspire, etc.)
3. Where do I get funding from the community for after-school and summer programing?
   a. Lions Club
   b. Optimist Club
   c. Grants, private donations, etc.
4. Where do you go for help with training community staff?
   a. Parents
   b. PE/APE Teacher
   c. PE/APE Consultants (college professors)
   d. Paraeducators
   e. Coaches
5. Who can help you to teach the children how to advocate for their needs?
   a. PE/APE teacher
   b. Parents
   c. Coaches
   d. Classroom Teachers
   e. Specialists
      i. Physical Therapist
      ii. Vision Teacher
      iii. Autism Specialist
      iv. Occupational Therapist
      v. School Psychologist
      vi. Peers

AFTER-SCHOOL PROGRAMS AND THE LAW: WHAT ARE STUDENTS' RIGHTS?

In this section we will discuss and clarify what are the rights of individuals with disabilities in relation to after-school programs and community participation. Further we will clarify the responsibilities of school districts and communities in terms of providing equal opportunities to individuals with disabilities.

The purposes of these legislations are to provide equal opportunities to individuals with disabilities in areas like sports and recreational activities that had been neglected in school settings and community programs.

Arnhold, Young, & Lakowski (2013) described the January 24 of 2013 Office of Civil Rights document titled "Dear Colleague Letter," which purpose is to clarify school obligations to provide extracurricular athletic opportunities for students with disabilities. It clarified the existing obligations of school districts to provide equal participation opportunities to children with disabilities in extracurricular activities like athletics, clubs, and intramurals.

The letter also points out the responsibility of school districts in four areas: (1) review of the general legal requirements of the Rehab Act of 1973-Section 504, (2) reminder that we cannot rely on generalizations and stereotypes, (3) the use of strong language in ensuring equal opportunities in after-school athletics and sports, and (4) the offering of separate or different athletic opportunities if reasonable accommodations and supplementary aids and services were still not enough to provide effective participation (Davis, 2013) (see figure 4.2).

Further, they described that the letter encouraged schools to comply with their responsibilities under Section 504 of the Rehabilitation Act of 1973, which states

> *that no otherwise qualified individual with a disability in the United States shall,* **_solely by reason of her or his disability_**, *be excluded from the participation in, be denied the benefits of, or be subjected to discrimination under **any program or activity** receiving Federal financial assistance.*

This letter provided guidance to districts and clarifies when and how schools must include students with disabilities in mainstream athletic

---

A school district must ...

- provide students with disabilities an equal opportunity to participate in its existing extracurricular athletic programs.
- makes an individualized inquiry to determine if there are reasonable modifications or necessary aids and services that would allow a student with a disability the chance to take part in the activity.

A school district must provide equal opportunity for participation...

- making reasonable modifications (policies, practices, or procedures).
- providing aids and services that are necessary.
- ensuring safe participation.
- unless modifications constitute a fundamental alteration of nature of the activity.

Student with disability have the right to.....

- have accommodations during try outs.
- be selected or cut from the team solely on ability level not disability.
- have alternatives in case they do not make the team (unified or separate sport teams).

Figure 4.2

programs. Further, it defines what equal treatment of student athletes with disabilities is, and encourages and provides guidance to schools on how to create adapted programs for students with disabilities.

Another legislation that is worth mentioning is Americans with Disability Act (ADA 101-336 1990). This legislation states that private entities in the public eye cannot discriminate against people with disabilities and must make reasonable accommodations in employment, state and local government, public accommodations, and telecommunications. It also looks at private, nonreligious schools, sports clubs, and all places that public schools go or use.

HOW CAN WE MAKE THIS HAPPEN?

Collaboration between School, District, and Community

Collaboration between school and community is extremely important for the effective participation of children and youth with disabilities in after-school sport and recreation programs (Davis, 2013). Literature suggests that there are many benefits when individuals with disabilities are socially included in their communities. One big first step is to promote the participation of extracurricular sport and recreational activities.

For example, Cappuccio (2013) developed a new sport league for children with disabilities with approximately 3,000 students governed by the Wisconsin Interscholastic Athletic Association. He offered an explanation of the steps he followed to establish a good relationship with the Special Education Department office in his school district and how he was able to fund and create his program. The steps he followed are given below.

1. *Preparation and Homework*: he suggests contacting parents and caregivers to see their interest and commitment. Then go to the local school district with parents support and present the program proposal clarifying your purpose and rationale which should be the need to create equitable and fair extracurricular athletics to students with disabilities as mandated by sections 504 and dear colleague letter.
2. *Presentation to the School Board*: should present the value of extracurricular athletics for all students, and evidence the lack of programming and disconnection of students with disabilities and their parents currently experience in school related to sport. Emphasize the benefits of positive physical and social outcomes for this group of students and their families.
3. *Details for Proposal*: detail what is needed to be able to make this happen. It is suggested to take into consideration offering this alternative using

the same format as traditional school district sport programs. It should be provided through the entire school year involving both boys and girls and sponsored with school district funds that will come from the extra-curricular budget (including pay for coaches, uniforms, equipment and transportation).

As mentioned by Cappucio (2013) it is extremely important to have parents' and guardians' involvement in this process. Parents and guardians are the most important advocates for their children with disabilities. For this reason it is imperative to follow Norlin's (2006) advice when he said that federal laws entitles children with disabilities to participate in extracurricular activities and this will likely not happen unless parents get actively involved in making this part of their child's IEP.

INCLUDE AFTER-SCHOOL PROGRAM PARTICIPATION ON THE STUDENTS' IEP & 504 PLANS

Another way that general and adapted physical educators can help students with disabilities in their transition process to the community is by including after-school sport objectives as part of their transition planning.

In every student IEP, there is a section for transition planning to be completed once they reach age sixteen, or earlier if determined by the IEP team. This transition planning must include appropriate measurable postsecondary goals based upon age-appropriate transition assessments related to education/ training, employment, and independent living.

Further it must state the transition services needed to assist the child reaching those goals, which are instruction, related services, community experiences (leisure and recreation skills), development of employment and other post school adult living objectives, acquisition of daily living skills and functional vocational assessment.

Clearly, it is recommended that after-school sports be an integral part of the community experience in leisure and recreation skills to be developed for an effective transition.

TRAINING COMMUNITY PERSONNEL, VOLUNTEERS, ADMINISTRATORS, AND STAFF HOW TO INCLUDE CHILDREN WITH DISABILITIES INTO THEIR PROGRAMS

Last but not least, one of the key elements to make the inclusion of students with disabilities in extracurricular sport and after-school programs will be

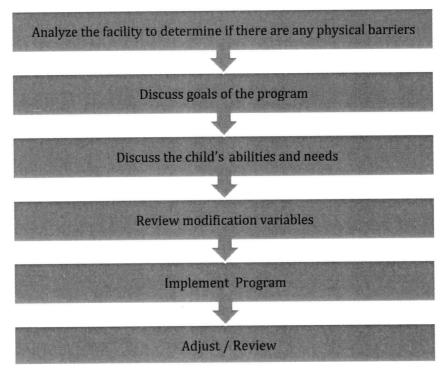

Figure 4.3

to provide training to all personnel involved in this process. From parents to administrators to staff and volunteers both in school and community, training must occur. Each child is unique and with different ability levels and needs. Here we provide some steps to consider when conducting training (figure 4.3).

Note:

- Consultant services, one-day workshops with follow-ups, skype consultations and others can be done with some careful planning and reciprocal communication.
- If appropriate, include parents and the child in the process.

SUMMARY

The purpose of this chapter was to provide parents and any other personnel working with students with disabilities with important information and ideas on how to effectively provide after-school sport and recreational opportunities for this population. It is important to understand that we need to continue to advocate for this population of students so their voice can be heard and they can have equal access to sport and recreational activities within and outside school settings.

By doing this, we are also advocating for a better and more effective transition to the community which is the ultimate goal, to make sure every person with a disability can be active members of this society in a satisfactory and safe manner.

It is very important to remember that this is all about creating equal opportunities for children and youth with disabilities and we must be creative. It is also important to remember that when making placement decisions related to sport and recreation, we should not judge before conducting an assessment and determine the student/athlete level of performance. Remember that team participation should be based on students' abilities, not disabilities.

Finally, if you are a professional that has students with disabilities in your school setting and need assistance, ask for help! Adapted physical educators, related service personnel, therapeutic recreation specialists can provide you with some insights on how to work and effectively integrate any student with a disability, and follow the guidelines provided in this chapter for a successful program.

REFERENCES

Americans with Disabilities Act of 1990, Pub. L. No. 101-336, §2, 104 Stat. 328 (1991).

Arnhold, R., Young, L. & Lakowski, T. (2013). Helping general physical educators and adapted physical educators address the Office of Civil Rights Dear Colleague Guidance Letter: The historical and legal background leading to the Office of Civil Rights "Dear Colleague Letter." *Journal of Physical Education, Recreation and Dance* 84:8, 20–23.

Cappuccio (2013). Helping general physical educators and adapted physical educators address the Office of Civil Rights Dear Colleague Guidance Letter: How one Wisconsin school district is moving forward while addressing the OCR Guidance . *Journal of Physical Education, Recreation and Dance* 84:8, 34–35.

Davis, R. (2013). Helping general physical educators and adapted physical educators address the Office of Civil Rights Dear Colleague Guidance Letter. *Journal of Physical Education, Recreation and Dance* 84:8, 19.

Deci, E. L. & Ryan, R. M. (1985). *Intrinsic motivation and self-determination in human behavior*. New York: Plenum.

Hodge, S. R., Lieberman, L. & Murratta, N. (2012). *Essentials of teaching adapted physical education: Diversity, culture and inclusion*. Holcomb Publishers, Scottsdale, Arizona.

National Longitudinal Transition Study 2, (2005). Retrieved on January, 2015 from: http://www.nlts2.org/reports/index.html.

National Organization on Disability (2010). *Survey of Americans with disabilities.* Washington D.C.: Author. Retrieved on January 15, 2015 from: http://www.2010 disabilitysurveys.org/indexold.html.

Norlin, J. (2006). *Athletics, extracurricular activities, and students with disabilities: District obligations under IDEA and Section 504.* Horsham, PA: LRP. Rehabilitation Act of 1973, Pub. L. No. 93-112, 87 Stat. 355.

Samalot-Rivera, A., Aleman, A. & Volmar, V. (2015). Increasing transition opportunities for youth with disabilities: Existing successful programs and steps to follow in program selection. *JOPERD Teaching Tips* (in press).

U.S. Department of Education Office for Civil Rights. (January 25, 2013). *Dear Colleague Letter—Extracurricular athletics for students with disabilities.* Retrieved from: http://www2.ed.gov/about/offices/list/ocr/letters/colleague-201301-504.pdf.

U.S. Government Accountability Office (2010). Students with disabilities: More information and guidance could improve opportunities in physical education and athletics. Report to Congressional Requesters. Retrieved on January 15, 2015 from: http://www.gao.gov/assets/310/305770.pdf.

Wagner, M., Newman, L., Cameto, R., Garza, N. & Levine, P. (2005). After high school: A first look at the postschool experiences of youth with disabilities. *A Report from the National Longitudinal Transition Study-2 (NLTS2).* Menlo Park, CA: SRI International. Available at www.nlts2.org/reports/2005_04/nlts2_report_2005_04_complete.pdf.

Chapter 5

What Every Parent Should Know about Equal Rights for Students with Disabilities Participating in Interscholastic Athletics and Sports

Garth Tymeson and Ronald Davis

Cole is a fifteen-year-old student with autism spectrum disorder (ASD) who receives special education and related services and participates with his non-disabled peers on their high school cross-country team. As an elementary student, Cole enjoyed playing the game of tag; he just never seemed to get tired of playing. Cole's first exposure to school-sponsored extracurricular activities was in sixth grade. His parents remembered how much he liked running while playing tag so at his Individual Education Program (IEP) meeting for transitioning from elementary to middle school, his parents requested that he participate in cross country to enhance his social skills and health behaviors.

This chapter is about one idea: helping parents with children with disabilities understand their children should be guaranteed opportunities to participate in school-sponsored extracurricular athletics. Our intent is to provide a simple, easy-to-follow "road map" for parents to help navigate through the twists and turns of working collaboratively with school district's special education programs and other service deliveries to obtain equal rights for all students' participation in school-sponsored extracurricular athletics.

We will start with a legislative foundation covering a brief review of two key federal laws: Section 504 of PL 93-112 (Rehabilitation Act of 1973) and the Individuals with Disabilities Education Act (IDEA). After the legislative foundation, we will present an "update" related to PL 93-112, Sec 504 activity.

Recently, the U.S. Congress, the U.S. Department of Education (USDE), the Government Accountability Office (GAO), and the Office of Civil Rights (OCR) released a "Dear Colleague Letter," which was focused on the participation rights of students with disabilities (SWD) in extracurricular athletics.

Parents should be aware of this letter and should ask about this Dear Colleague Letter at their child's next IEP meeting.

We plan to use short vignettes to tell true stories of students with disabilities and their family's actions and advocacy while engaged in obtaining appropriate special educational programming, including extracurricular athletics. Tables, charts, and diagrams will be used to help parents track the proper steps and pathways to follow before, during, and after IEP meetings, which should be used to secure extracurricular athletics programming on your child's IEP.

We will share model school-based extracurricular athletic programs from around the United States. In addition, we will offer an inclusive sports integration model and identify current trends in sports such as NCAA-recognized collegiate competition for students with disabilities.

LEGISLATIVE FOUNDATION

This section will provide a brief overview of two key federal laws that mandate support and educational opportunity for students with disabilities. These laws are

- Section 504 of Public Law 93–112 and Section 504 entitled the Rehabilitation Act of 1973.
- The IDEA (1975); (IDEIA, 2004, was passed in 2004 = IDEA 2004; final rules and regulations were published in 2006).*

PUBLIC LAW (PL) 93-112—THE REHABILITATION ACT OF 1973, SECTION 504

The Rehabilitation Act of 1973 is commonly referred to as the first civil rights law for persons with disabilities. In particular, Section 504 of this law states that "no otherwise qualified individual with a disability in the United States shall, solely by reason of her or his disability, be excluded from the participation in, be denied the benefits of, or be subjected to discrimination under any program or activity receiving Federal financial assistance." (29 U.S.C. §794 et seq. [Rehabilitation Act, 1973]).

In other words, your son or daughter cannot be denied the opportunity to engage in a school-sponsored extracurricular activity (e.g., athletics or sports) solely based on their disability. You will read later that some form of assessment must be conducted to determine eligibility to an extracurricular sports

---

* For purposes of this chapter, IDEA will be used as reference.

team other than their impairment (i.e., meeting a qualifying time for a track event).

You may be thinking—*Ron, I don't understand what this previous sentence is getting at? What's the point?* Here's an example:

THE INDIVIDUALS WITH DISABILITIES EDUCATION ACT (IDEA)

The IDEA was first passed in 1975 and most recently reauthorized in 2004 for the purpose of providing free appropriate public school education (FAPE) in the least restrictive environment (LRE) for children 0–3 and 3–21 as determined by an appropriate diagnostic instrument in one or more of the following areas: physical and cognitive development, communication, social or emotional development, or adaptive development. Results from an assessment could determine if the student is eligible for special education and related services to enhance their educational program.

This process of determining appropriate education services is conducted by trained school district personnel, recorded, and submitted for parental agreement during an IEP meeting. Documentation of assessment results, suggested programing, timelines for initiation and duration of services, goals and objectives, and other aspects are recorded in the IEP document.

The IEP document is a binding agreement of educational services between parents and school districts; parents need to give this document considerable thought before signing.

Parents need to consider the extracurricular needs of their child when preparing for and meeting with their child's IEP team. Extracurricular services and activities are part of all students' educational experience, and should be documented, where appropriate on the IEP. Figure 5.1 shows how IDEA defines extracurricular activities. Notice that the definition includes athletics.

DEFINING CHILD WITH A DISABILITY ACCORDING TO SEC 504 VERSUS IDEA

Parents must understand that every child who is considered a "student with a disability" as defined by IDEA is protected by Section 504; but some students with disabilities covered under Sec 504 are not considered students with disabilities under IDEA. Remember IDEA is established to provide free and appropriate public education based on educational assessments that helps determine the least restrictive environment for learning. (i.e., assessment process of the IEP).

Section 300.107 Nonacademic Services: The state must ensure the following:

(a)   Each public agency must take steps, including the provision of supplementary aids and services determined appropriate and necessary by the child's IEP Team, to provide nonacademic and extracurricular services and activities in the manner necessary to afford children with disabilities an equal opportunity for participation in those services and activities.

(b)   Nonacademic and extracurricular services and activities may include counseling services, athletics, transportation, health services, recreational activities, special interest groups or clubs sponsored by the public agency, referrals to agencies that provide assistance to individuals with disabilities, and employment of students, including both employment by the public agency and assistance in making outside employment available.

Page 46763 of Federal Register—Monday, August 14, 2006 Final Rules and Regulations for IDEA 2004 at: http://www2.ed.gov/legislation/FedRegister/finrule/2006-3/081406a.pdf

Figure 5.1

PL 93-112, Sec 504 is about providing a student with a disability "accommodations" for success (i.e., large print textbook, ramps to classrooms or gymnasiums). Generally, students with disabilities under Sec 504 have grade-level academic performance and are not in need of "instructional" interventions.

Students receiving support under Sec 504 should have a written Section 504 Plan, which should be filed with the school district. The Section 504 Plan is not a required document, and is school district specific. Parents should be knowledgeable of such a plan and you should ask to meet with your school district's 504 Coordinator to explain the document and the services provided. Students needing a specially designed plan (i.e., those considered obese, low motor coordination, poor posture) may have such a plan delivered by an adapted physical educator (APE).

See table 5.1 for comparison of PL 93-112 and IDEA regarding extracurricular athletics.

AN UPDATE RELATED TO PL 93-112, SEC 504 AND THE DEAR COLLEAGUE LETTER TO SCHOOL DISTRICTS REGARDING EXTRACURRICULAR SCHOOL-BASED ACTIVITIES

Between 2008 and 2011 Congress requested an investigation by the Government Accounting Office (GAO) on the availability of athletic opportunities for students with disabilities in schools in the form of review and evaluation

Table 5.1   Comparison of PL 93-112-Sec 504, and IDEA Related to Extracurricular Athletics

	PL 93-112	IDEA
Defines SWD	Broadly defined as physical and mental impairments	Specific and requires assessment to determine educational need
Ages of children	School age and beyond	0–3, and 3–21
Addresses Physical Education as service	No	Yes
Includes Extracurricular sports/athletics	Yes	Yes
Do all SWD require services under IDEA?	No	Yes
Creates a legal contract with parents and school district to deliver identified programming	No (504 plan is not required) but once plan is developed these services must be provided	Yes with IEP
Is there a mechanism to assure athletic opportunity would be provided?	No (optional for school districts to have a 504 plan)	Yes, via extracurricular services and activities
Provides accommodations to benefit from school-based programs to include extracurricular sports/activities	Yes	Yes

Initial event	2008 Congress Issues Charge to GAO to Assess Current Status of students with disabilities (SWD) in Physical Education and Sport
Result event	2010 GAO Reported back to Congress
Final event	2011 As a result of the GAO findings U.S. Department of Education Charges Office of Civil Rights (OCR) to issue **2013 The Dear Colleague Letter sent to all school districts and state departments of education (*this letter is not an official mandate to the schools, but a guidance document that clarifies existing federal laws and regulations.**

Figure 5.2

of how Sec 504 was being implemented in schools. Data were also collected on physical education programming for students with disabilities.

The chain of events for this report is presented in figure 5.2. As you read through this diagram, keep in mind that these Congressional actions are based on the legislative foundation of PL 93-112, and Sec 504, previously discussed in this chapter.

GAO FINDINGS REPORTED TO CONGRESS

The GAO identified several factors that limit opportunities for students with disabilities to participate in physical education and athletics and produced the following recommendations to school districts:

1. *Accessibility* (address the environment)
2. *Equipment* (safe and effective use of sport equipment)
3. *Personnel Preparation* (training highly qualified APE teachers and coaches)
4. *Teaching Style* (adapting individualized teaching techniques)
5. *Management of Behavior* (coaches need appropriate behavior management skills)
6. *Program Options* (alternative, adapted, and appropriate sport opportunities)
7. *Curriculum* (adapted, accessible curricula to meet needs of students with disabilities)
8. *Assessment, Progress, Achievement*

The GAO study found that schools in the states reviewed provide students with and without disabilities similar opportunities in physical education and extracurricular athletics, but teachers and coaches have serious challenges in offering these opportunities for students with disabilities (lack of training, equipment, facilities, budget, etc.).

The GAO determined that students with disabilities who participate in extracurricular sports did so through school-based programs or community-based teams. Finally, the GAO suggested that the USDE (Department) provides only marginal support and guidance in both areas assessed (sports and physical education) to schools for students with disabilities.

SO HOW DOES THE GAO REPORT AND DEAR COLLEAGUE LETTER AFFECT ME AS PARENT OF A CHILD WITH A DISABILITY WHO MAY WANT TO PARTICIPATE IN EXTRACURRICULAR ATHLETICS?

The information presented in the Dear Colleague Letter, which was sent to all special education directors and athletic directors in the United States, helped to clarify the responsibilities of school districts and outlined 4 key areas as presented in table 5.2.

The following vignettes provide real situations of how parents have collaborated with school districts to obtain extracurricular athletics services for their children with disabilities. Important aspects of each of these true stories

Table 5.2   Results of GAO Report and Suggestions for Parents

School District Responsibilities as Identified by the Dear Colleague Letter	*What Parents Should Do*
It reviewed the general legal requirements of the Rehabilitation Act of 1973-Section 504 that should be in place for all school districts.	Ask if your district received a copy of the Dear Colleague Letter from January 2013. If not, provide them with a copy. Ask to talk with the Section 504 Coordinator in the district.
It reminded school officials that determination for membership to athletic teams, or opportunities to join such teams cannot rely on disability generalizations and stereotypes	Ask the coach, athletic director, or leader for a copy of the evaluation criteria to join an athletic team. Recognize that your child has the right to access; he or she must perform high enough to make the squad or team just as another student without a disability does
Provided strong language in ensuring equal opportunities in after-school athletics and sports	Again, realize your child should have "equal opportunity," but this is not a guarantee to making the team
URGED the offering of separate or adapted athletic opportunities if reasonable accommodations and supplementary aids and services were still not enough to provide effective participation with nondisabled peers in general athletic program.	Establishing a separate or different athletic opportunity is not required by these findings. However, this is where discussion during your IEP meetings could take place. Getting sports programming on your child's IEP or Sec 504 Plan would be very important to address this finding. See vignettes below for more ideas.

are how the services are specifically documented on the IEP and Section 504 Plan and how the parents can act as real team members and collaborate with the IEP team and with the school's Section 504 coordinator.

Cole

Cole is a fifteen-year-old student with ASD who receives special education services and successfully participates with his nondisabled peers on their high school cross-country team. Diagnosed with ASD at age four, he is affectionate, creative, and full of energy, but has challenges with anxiety, communicating, and social relationships.

As an elementary student, Cole's parents found that one technique that helped him interact with his peers was by starting a game of tag. This physical activity seemed to reduce his anxiety as he laughed and talked while playing tag with other kids. Many kids would comment about how tired they were because Cole just never seemed to get tired of playing. It appeared that he was a natural runner who enjoyed being physically active.

Cole's trek to this point in his interscholastic athletic career is one that many parents of students with disabilities can learn from to obtain school-sponsored extracurricular athletics for their children in special education. This includes the important aspects of parents working in a positive collaborative manner, requesting these services, and having extracurricular activity participation listed on the IEP like all other special education services.

Cole's parents were proactive in their approach to collaborating with school district special education staff to receive these services. Cole's first exposure to school-sponsored extracurricular activities was during his first year of middle school in sixth grade. His parents remembered how much he liked running while playing tag with other kids.

They also recognized his need, as he got older, to have more interactions with his peers, to feel positive and confident about himself, to be healthy and physically active, and they knew that physical education and extracurricular activities were part of required special education services. Therefore, at his IEP meeting for transitioning from fifth to sixth grade (elementary to middle school), his parents requested that he participate in cross-country running, an extracurricular activity that matched his abilities and interests.

Content was included on his IEP at this meeting. In addition, six months later as the fall season approached, another IEP meeting was held to confirm specifics about his extracurricular participation. Below is the content from the middle school IEP.

> An IEP meeting was held on 8/19/11 to discuss Cole's access to and involvement in extracurricular activities. At Cole's IEP meeting dated 2/25/11, it was discussed as a team to have Cole participate in cross country just before entering Middle School (grade 6). At this time, the IEP team decided that it would be beneficial to have Cole participate with the assistance of an adult mentor to ensure Cole's safety, motivation, and clear understanding of the cross country running expectations.
>
> However, the IEP team did not go into detail as to how this would work. The IEP team convened on 8/19/11 and determined that Cole would need support of an additional adult to fully access the cross-country program, to motivate him, and ensure his physical safety and full understanding of the expectations, which would be provided under the direct supervision of an educational assistant (EA).
>
> This determination was made due to the unique setting that cross country is in, not be fully contained or always clearly marked for the runners to rely upon. The IEP team also determined that if at any time Cole's anxiety becomes so overwhelming that he is not able to fully participate in the practice or meet that the coach and EA will collaborate and make a determination at that time as to whether Cole needs to be removed from the practice/meet, this will then be communicated to Cole's parents.

> Cole will travel on the bus with his team to meets and his EA will meet him on site. No services are needed for transportation at this time.

Cole's initial participation on the middle school cross-country team was successful, but challenging. The coach was supportive and truly enjoyed having Cole on the team. An important support provided to Cole during his three middle school cross-country seasons was a local college student running with him as an educational assistant, or as Cole called him—his "coach."

This supplemental aid provided frequent and necessary visual and verbal guidance while running and participating in other aspects of practice and competition. Cole loved being at practice with the other kids, but the large number of runners, the sounds of the starting gun, cheering fans, and chaos at the finish line chute were all difficult for him to manage.

To accommodate his individual needs during meets, he would run with the help of his "coach." This "coach" served as an EA who assisted Cole with all aspects needed for completion of the running course. For the first couple of years in middle school, Cole would be very anxious while running and would firmly grasp the arm of his paraprofessional while running. Gradually he gained enough self-confidence to run without this physical contact.

In order for Cole to participate in actual meets with his EA, the athletic director requested a waiver from the State Athletic Association. Below is what was obtained from the State Association to facilitate Cole's successful participation in middle school meets.

> The WIAA will waive the National Federation Cross Country Rule 9-7-4 allowing Cole M. to have a guide run with him to offer assistance. This waiver is given for middle school level competition only. It will be the responsibility of your coach to carry a copy of this letter and show it to the WIAA officials and the opposing coach at the premeet conference.

When it was time for Cole to transition from eighth grade to high school, his parents had seen the benefits of cross-country participation and wanted this to continue as part of his special education program. In addition, Cole's self-confidence grew and he wanted to continue extracurricular participation in high school with his friends.

This participation was discussed at his IEP meeting the spring before his transition to high school, and the specifics were written on his IEP (see figure 5.3 below).

Cole now loves going to practice with his high school teammates, and is often seen smiling during practice. But racing in the meets can be a struggle for him since the high school distance is longer, the other runners are faster, and the crowds are larger and louder. Therefore, he still has a "coach" who runs with him.

Extracurricular and Non-academic Activities (This is for 9ᵗʰ grade)
Will the student be able to participate in extracurricular and nonacademic activities with
nondisabled students?

Yes   No

(If no, describe the extent to which the student will not be involved in extracurricular and
nonacademic activities with nondisabled students)
*Cole intends on participating in cross country in 9ᵗʰ grade. Cole has participated
successfully in cross country all of his middle school years. Cole does need the support
of an additional adult to fully access the cross-country team event. This additional adult
is there to motivate him, ease his social anxiety related to his autism, ensure his physical
safety by running the correct course, and make sure that Cole is fully aware of all
expectations. The IEP team concluded that if Cole's anxiety becomes too much to handle
in practice or a meet that Cole's parents will be contacted after that decision has been
made by the additional adult and coach. Cole will travel on the cross-country bus with
his team mates. Special transportation is not required at this time for meets.*

Figure 5.3

However, Cole has asked to run in the meets without his "coach." This
independence is a very positive step and provides Cole with much self-confidence among his peers. In order to have his paraprofessional guide continue
to provide necessary support, the athletic director again requested a waiver
from the State High School Interscholastic Athletic Association. Below is
content contained in this waiver.

The WIAA will waive the National Federation Cross Country Rule 9-7-4 allowing Cole Murphy to have a guide run with him to offer assistance within the
following parameters:

1. No restriction as to level of competition (varsity and/or sub-varsity),
2. Guide may use physical contact at the start of the race,
3. During the race, while on the course, guide runs behind athlete, may provide
   verbal cues, and
4. At the finish, limited contact, only as needed due to congestion.

Parents need to state their desire to have this extracurricular participation
content on the IEP. This IEP stipulates that extracurricular activities are a
required part of his special education services. The IEP form shown at the end
of this chapter is the Wisconsin Department of Public Instruction template
that is used by many districts.

The extracurricular requirement is addressed in Cole's IEP through his participation on the cross-country team. According to individual student needs,
interests, and abilities, there could be a wide range of possible extracurricular

activities based on existing offerings at the school or approved activities by the IEP team.

Whatever extracurricular activities parents feel would benefit the student, should be requested in writing and included on the IEP to document the services, including supplemental aids and services related to extracurricular activity participation.

Parents need to proactively seek out and request extracurricular athletic opportunities for their children through the special education IEP process. Cross country has helped Cole build self-confidence, has created more opportunities for him to interact with his peers to develop social skills, has made him feel a part of the school community, and has given him a sense of pride that he can do what the other kids do in high school.

Summary: As can be seen above, Cole's extracurricular athletic experience is properly documented on the IEP as part of his free appropriate public education required by federal special education law. When parents and school districts collaborate via the IEP team process, meaningful and beneficial student outcomes can occur via required extracurricular activities. See figure 5.1.

VIGNETTE OF SWD IN SEGREGATED/ADAPTED SPORT PROGRAM (MODERATE COGNITIVE AND MILD PHYSICAL DISABILITY)

Danny

Danny is a healthy and active sixteen-year-old high school student with moderate cognitive disability and a minor orthopedic impairment (mild cerebral palsy) that affects his calves, ankles, and feet. He has had several surgeries on his feet and ankles that have allowed him to independently run for safe and active participation in sport.

Danny receives most of his educational services in a special education class with other students having cognitive and/or physical disabilities. He participates in specially designed (adapted) physical education that is documented with present level of performance, annual goals/objectives, and frequency/duration of services on his IEP.

While in elementary and middle school, he participated in several community-based adapted sport programs such as basketball, baseball, and soccer conducted by the YMCA and local city Park and Recreation Association. Danny loves being around his peers and adults, and enjoys showing off his sport skills.

When Danny entered high school, his parents were interested in having him involved in extracurricular athletic activities like his older sibling and other students. However, due to Danny's cognitive disability he was not able to participate safely with his nondisabled peers on general sport teams due to the complex nature of strategies, concepts, and skills required. He needs extensive physical guidance and many visual demonstrations to follow directions for sport participation.

Knowing that participation in the general sport program for nondisabled students was not an appropriate placement for him, Danny's parents, along with several other parents of students in special education, approached the APE teachers and asked about school-sponsored athletic opportunities for their children that were comparable to those received by nondisabled students in the district.

The APE teachers reviewed the request, contacted other school districts, that offer adapted sport program, and proposed the idea to the high school athletic director, district special education director, and other school district administrators. The concept was supported and has resulted in an adapted sport league among three school districts in the area high school interscholastic athletic conference.

Danny and other student-athletes with a wide variety of disabilities now participate in a three-season, year-round extracurricular program, earn high school athletic letters, have paid coaches, and are part of the culture of extracurricular athletics in their public schools. This has provided many students who cannot safely or meaningfully participate with their nondisabled peers to benefit from a competitive extracurricular athletic experience.

The program in West Central Wisconsin is closely aligned with the Minnesota Interscholastic Adapted Sport model with rule adaptations to meet the needs of their schools and student-athletes. Danny and his peers now participate in indoor soccer, floor hockey, and baseball during high school years. Parents have requested this participation to be included on their students IEPs as indicated on the Wisconsin Department of Public Instruction IEP form (See figure 5.5).

SUMMARY OF VIGNETTES

These two vignettes provide parents with information on different forms of extracurricular athletics that benefit students with disabilities. One is inclusive participation with nondisabled peers that meets the needs of a student with autism. The other example of an adapted sport program provides extracurricular athletic opportunities for students with different learning needs, and provides meaningful educational outcomes.

The following is a vignette of a student considered to be a student with a disability as identified by PL 93-112, Section 504. Students identified as Sec

504 students are those who are broadly defined as having physical or mental impairments needing accommodations to successfully engage educational and extracurricular activities, that is, ramps to classrooms, assistive devices for improved mobility.

Educational needs for these students should be identified in a district 504 plan. Section 504 plans should be discussed with special education personnel and parents. It is likely some students receiving services under Sec 504 will not have an IEP, but require accommodations to appropriately engage educational and extracurricular activities. See table 5.3—Sample 504 Plan.

Nicole

Nicole is a first-year athlete with a single leg amputation. She uses two Canadian crutches to run, kick, jump, and move in sport activities. She has been competing on community teams, that is, swimming, soccer, basketball, for most of her life since age eight. But her first love is soccer.

Nicole participated in her traditional elementary and middle school physical education classes, and meets her high school eligibility based on academic merit (i.e., no cognitive delays). Nicole will be trying out for sports in her high school athletic program. Accommodations have been made to allow Nicole to use her crutches on the field during a soccer match.

Now as she enters High School, the State Interscholastic Athletic Association is questioning the safety of having Nicole on the field of play. During tryouts Nicole was required to complete all the same ball-handling drills and running requirements of all other athletes. She performed at the level of her nondisabled peers and met the team's requirements.

Accommodations for Nicole addressed rules for using her crutches for other than her locomotor needs. Basically she would not be allowed to use her crutches to pass, dribble, or shoot the ball; all ball movement would have to be completed by the action of her residual leg.

To address this rule and ensure safety for all players, Nicole was required to practice in parallel with the team for at least three weeks before being allowed to enter an official match. The parallel setting was used as an additional evaluation of her skills and determined an appropriate accommodation during match play. All this was documented on a Sec 504 Accommodation Plan from her school district.

In table 5.4 are steps parents should consider in planning to attend their child's IEP or Sec 504 Plan meeting. Take time to review and gather all necessary documentation prior to your visit. Remember, this should be a collaborative team effort to meet the needs of your child.

Table 5.3   Sample 504 Plan for Nicole

Name: Nicole	D.O.B.	Grade
School:	Meeting Date:	Comments:
Nature of the Concern Use of crutches during soccer match	*Comments*: Student is a single leg amputee with over 6 years' experience playing competitive soccer. Entering high school she has demonstrated above-average mobility and ball skills. Accommodations are requested to address rules for use of crutches to pass, dribble, or shoot the ball. All ball movement must be made in a traditional fashion, that is, with her residual leg and not with crutches	Does disability affect major life activities? There are limitations of movement. Crutches are required in all daily living activities related to locomotor, balance, and access of buildings, playing fields, and classrooms
Evaluations Completed Traditional Sprint, Dribbling, Passing and Shooting tests. Prior to the season, video performances of Nicole will be made available to the conference coaches to afford them the opportunity of seeing her play. Each opposing team's coaches will be allowed to evaluate the safety of the Nicole's presence on the field during competition Concerns will be addressed prior to the season on an individual basis as needed to the respective Athletic Directors.	*Student's Disability* Physical disability—leg amputation above knee	
List of Accommodations The student will be allowed to use her crutches to engage in the interscholastic sport of soccer at the secondary level. She will be a team member in parallel for a period of 3 weeks before entering a competitive game.	*Additional Accommodations* Should concerns arise that would prohibit Nicole from participating in a soccer match, on-site re-evaluations will be allowed and rule adjustments will be concerned prior to game play.	
Review and assessment date	Participants names	Official Signatures

Table 5.4   Suggested Steps for Parents to Follow in Preparation for IEP or Section 504 Meetings

Steps for parents preparing for IEP or Section 504 meetings to request extracurricular athletics:

1. Organize your materials in a file folder in preparation for your IEP and other school meetings. Don't be overwhelmed, ask others for help; have an advocate to help with this topic just like with other topics.
2. Have a copy of "Section 300.107 Nonacademic Services" listed in IDEA (see above) in your file. The explanation of extracurricular activities within special education is contained in Section 300.107. If necessary, this can be shared with members of the IEP team and others responsible for extracurricular services in the school district. Everyone needs to understand that extracurriculars are part of special education. You are only asking for what your child is entitled to under special education law.
3. Submit a request for the desired extracurricular services in writing at least a week prior to IEP meeting (see sample—"Request for Extracurricular Activities"). Bring a copy of that request to the meeting. Send this request to your child's special education teacher and the IEP case manager. (If necessary, follow-up with director of special education and athletics director.)
4. Familiarize yourself with the offerings in the extracurricular athletic program in the school district. These can be found on the district's website or you can request this information. The extracurricular activities will usually include sports and other offerings like clubs and special interest groups. Your child can benefit from this type of school-sponsored participation. Look at this list and determine what may be best for your child.
5. Request that the desired extracurricular services are listed on the IEP (or 504 Plan). Be sure this includes details regarding supplemental aids or services, waivers, or adaptations necessary for participation. Based on the individual student and sport, this could include additional staff or modified equipment, or may simply note the participation frequency and duration. If possible, offer suggestions to the school district about using local college, volunteers, etc.
6. If necessary, request that the school district ask for an interpretation from the state-level interscholastic athletic governing body for any of necessary supports or rule adaptations allowed for your child while participating in actual competition. This possible waiver would generally only apply if the SWD was participating with nondisabled peers in the general sport program competition.
7. Monitor your child's participation to be sure that the services are being provided as listed on the IEP (or 504 Plan). Offer any assistance you can provide to have a positive, proactive, and collaborative relationship with school staff who coach your child.
8. As a parent, be prepared to offer assistance with things like transportation, etc. Go to events for support; be on time to practice and at end, etc.

The following is a sample *Request for Extracurricular Activities* that can precede an IEP meeting and can be shared with the special education teacher (See figure 5.4).

Figure 5.5 is a sample IEP component form from the Wisconsin Department of Public Instruction. This form is offered as a model for parents to

Dear ____

The purpose of this memo is to request extracurricular athletic services for my daughter, Sarah, as part of her special education program. We are interested in having her participate on an adapted soccer team (or whatever sport is reasonable and feasible) since her disability does not allow for safe and successful participation on the high school soccer team with her nondisabled peers. We would like to discuss this participation and have these services listed on her IEP in the area "Participation in Extracurricular and Nonacademic Activities."

Thank you for your work with Sarah. We look forward to discussing the addition of school-sponsored extracurricular athletic services for Sarah. We feel this an important part of her individualized education program.
Thank you

_____

Figure 5.4

review to become familiar with the various sections and components. Each state has their own variation of an IEP form but all states and school districts must include components in the federal IDEA law, including extracurricular services and activities.

SUMMARY

The intent of this chapter was to provide a simple, easy-to-follow "road map" for parents of students with disabilities to help navigate a school district's special education program and other services, especially those involving participation in school-sponsored extracurricular athletics. Parents are encouraged to prepare for their IEP or Section 504 plan meetings and be ready to address their child's needs for extracurricular and nonacademic activities (i.e., athletics). Documentation of extracurricular services and activities should be a part of their child's IEP to include goals/objectives and supports in these areas.

Parents need to ask for key documents and seek explanations of how their child is being provided equal opportunity to engage in athletic teams. Parents should ask for copies of the OCR "Dear Colleague Letter" dated January 2013, and they should ask to speak with the Section 504 Coordinator and inquire about how the services listed on an IEP in the area "Participation in Extracurricular and Nonacademic Activities" are being addressed for their child. Parents who take time to prepare for IEP or Section 504 plan meetings will help everyone involved develop better service delivery for their child.

Form I-9 (Rev. 10/06) Name of Student _____

Projected beginning and ending date(s) of IEP services & modifications _____ to _____ *(month/day/year)*

   (month/day/year)

Physical education: □ **Regular**   □ **Specially designed**

Vocational education: □ Regular   □ Specially designed

Include a statement for each of I, II, III and IV below to allow the student (1) to advance appropriately toward attaining the annual goals; (2) to be involved and progress in the general education curriculum; (3) to be educated and participate with other students with and without disabilities to the extent appropriate, and (4) to participate in extracurricular and other nonacademic activities. Include frequency, location, & duration (if different from IEP beginning and ending dates).

I. Special education	Frequency/ Amount	Location	Duration

II. Related_services needed to benefit from special education including frequency,
   location, and duration *(if different from IEP beginning and ending dates).*

□ None needed to benefit from special education

                                                        Freq / Amt   Location
         Duration

	Freq / Amt	Location	Duration
□ Assistive Technology			
□ Audiology			
□ Counseling			
□ Educational Interpreting			
□ Medical Services for Diagnosis and Evaluation			
□ Occupational Therapy			
□ Orientation and Mobility (VI only)			
□ Physical Therapy			
□ Psychological Services			
□ Recreation			
□ Rehabilitation Counseling Services			
□ School Health Services			
□ School Nurse Services			
□ School Social Work Services			
□ Speech / Language			
□ Transportation			
□ Other: specify			
III. Supplementary aids and services: aids, services, and other supports provided to or on behalf of the student in regular education or other educational settings. □ Yes □ No *(If yes, describe)*	Freq / Amt	Location	Duration
IV. Program modifications or supports for school personnel that will be provided.			

Figure 5.5

Better preparation will help address the mandates put in place by the Rehabilitation Act of 1973 and IDEA and guard against their child being denied the opportunity to engage in a school-sponsored extracurricular activity (e.g., athletics or sports) solely based on their disability.

REFERENCES

U.S. Department of Education, Office for Civil Rights. (2013). *Dear Colleague.* Washington, DC: Author. Retrieved from: http://sped.dpi.wi.gov/sped_forms06.

Tymeson, G., (2013). What every parent should know about equal rights for students with disabilities participating in interscholastic athletics and sports. *Journal of Physical Education*, Recreation, Dance. 84(8).

Chapter 6

Utilizing Instructional Strategies for Increased Participation in School and Community Programs

Ellen Kowalski, Linda Webbert, and Rocco Aiello

Chad has autism and is ten years old. He attends his community public school and receives special education services, including adapted physical education. He has limited verbal communication. Chad's older brother who is twelve participates in the community soccer league. Chad usually attends his brother's practices and games with his parents, as a spectator.

At a parent teacher conference, Chad's physical education teacher commented that Chad has good fitness levels and sport skills, and that he can throw, catch, and dribble a basketball. He shows a real interest in using his feet to dribble and likes kicking a ball toward a target.

Chad's Dad asked the physical education teacher if he thought that Chad could play soccer, like his brother. The physical education teacher said that typically he would not recommend soccer, a team sport, for a student with autism; however, given Chad's fitness and skill levels, his interest, and that his brother could practice at home with him, in this case, he would give Chad the opportunity.

He gave the parents some tips and strategies that he used in class and stressed that for this to work, it would be important to work closely with a coach. Chad's Dad said he would love to help with the coach, but was not sure what he should be doing or how he can help Chad be successful on a team. The physical education teacher suggested some strategies the Dad could share with the coach, for example:

- *Using diagrams, pictures and video clips of skills, offensive and defensive strategies to use for practices and game play*
- *Showing Chad a stop watch with the amount of time for a game*
- *Having a red card to show him when he is to come out of the game for substitution and a green card for when he should be in the game*

71

- *Deciding on a signal he can use with the coach and with other players if he wants to come out of the game*
- *Practicing skills at home and setting up a goal for him to shoot*
- *Using a whistle for practice to stop and go*

The physical education teacher also recommended preparing the teammates and soliciting their help in making this a positive experience for everyone on the team.

When it was time for soccer sign ups, Chad was registered and his Dad contacted the coach and explained the situation. The coach, although apprehensive, was willing to try. Chad attended the first practice and in the beginning it was difficult to get him to practice the drills with the team. Sometimes he would participate in a drill and other times he would go off on his own just dribbling on the sideline.

With encouragement from his teammates he eventually participated in the entire practices and in game play. When it was time for the first game, Chad started, and although he never actually touched the ball, as no one intentionally passed to him, he ran up and down the field with the other players. He played a total of about seven minutes, but was engaged in watching and cheering for his team.

For the next game the coach told a few of the boys that they must try to pass the ball to Chad. He received a pass and dribbled toward the goal, but then lost the ball. In each game there was a slight improvement in his playing ability and in his teammates including him. There were obstacles along the way too. One time he became angry when he was pushed by an opposing player and walked off the field, another time he picked up the ball and threw it, and he yelled at the referee when he was called for a handball. But he finished the season, received his participation trophy and had his picture with the team. Chad's family was pleased with the overall experience and Chad has indicated he wants to play again.

BENEFITS FROM PARTICIPATING IN SPORT AND RECREATIONAL ACTIVITIES

There are many benefits from participating in recreational and sport activities. For all children, being involved in a sport or recreation provides opportunities to

- learn new skills
- increase physical fitness levels
- relieve stress

- help with sleeping
- build self-esteem
- socialize with peers
- build self-esteem and confidence
- have fun

All children should have the opportunity to experience the many benefits of being involved in sport and recreational activities. While there are many organized recreation athletic and sport programs such as Little League, gymnastics, karate, soccer, dance, lacrosse, and swimming available for normal children, this isn't necessarily true for children with disabilities.

The availability of recreational and sport programs designed for children with disabilities are not as prevalent or as easily accessible as they are for typical peers. Many of the sport and recreation programs for children with disabilities are designed for a specific disability, possibly making them inappropriate for children who have another type of disability.

When selecting a sport or activity, it is most important to first consider both the interests and disability of the child. For example, with Chad, his physical education teacher stated that he would not have recommended soccer as an activity for a child with autism. Team sports are typically difficult for a child with autism because of the constant change, multiple interactions, and social skills required to play.

However, Chad really loved soccer! With Chad's skills, interest in playing soccer, the assistance from the physical education teacher, and help at home from his brother, Chad's family made the decision to have him try the soccer team.

With awareness, training, and most importantly, a willingness to include children of all abilities, a child with disabilities can be successfully included and can participate in regular recreational activity programs with adaptations and modifications. Parents, coaches, and volunteers may not be aware of the many strategies that can be implemented which allow the child to be successful and enjoy participating in activities.

It is important to keep in mind that making modifications or adaptations should not change the intent of the game, but rather allow all children to participate in the game regardless of their ability. It is not about winning or losing, it is about playing!

To help you assist your child to become involved in community programs, an important person to establish good communication with is the child's physical education teacher. If possible, meet with the physical educator (during parent/teacher conferences is best) to discuss the child's IEP or physical education goals (Alexander & Schwager, 2012) as well as ways to help them become involved in community programs.

Not only can they help provide ideas for modifications and adaptations related to sport but they can give insight about the child's sensitivities, needs, and behavior in a large group environment and about various types of activities that parents may not have observed.

This is particularly true when selecting the community program if the child does not have siblings or many peers in the home environment. The physical educator can be particularly helpful when matching the activity with the interests and disability of the child.

Sometimes a child with a disability within the family unit can experience stress and anxiety, especially when it comes to doing activities that come more easily to their brother or sister. However, helping the sibling to be a peer assistant can enhance the experience for everyone. Being a peer assistant can offer support, become more resilient in dealing with a child with a disability experiences, and take pride in their brother or sister's achievements.

In this chapter, parents and coaches will be provided with practical information on how to assist a child with a disability to participate in physical activities, either in the community or when playing at home. Information in this chapter includes general considerations, a variety of instructional strategies, activities, modifications and adaptations and the appropriate time for teaching and coaching a child with a disability.

Also discussed are benefits of having siblings and school-age friends as peer assistants, assisting parents with ideas of how to be proactive when deciding to register their child in a community program.

INSTRUCTIONAL STRATEGIES

Many strategies and techniques that are used by physical educators can also be used by parents and coaches. Children with disabilities may need various types and levels of assistance in order to experience success while participating in physical activity. Based on how much support the child needs there are different types and levels of assistance that can be very helpful for parents and coaches to use.

Below is a description with specific examples of how a parent, a coach, or peer assistants would effectively provide the appropriate verbal cues, physical assistance, and feedback.

Verbal Cues

Verbal cues are one or two words that can be used by the coach or peer to tell the child what to do or to remind him or her how to perform a movement.

Examples:

"Sara, throw the ball."
"Ricky, it's your turn to bat."
"Let's stand on the black circle."
"Shane, stand next to this cone and kick the ball."

Modeling

Modeling is a way of demonstrating how to do the activity. After you give a verbal cue, if the student does not do the activity, or does the activity wrong, you should repeat the cue and demonstrate what it is you want him or her to do. This helps the child see what you want him or her to do.

Examples:

"Vashon, throw the ball like this."
"You need to swing level, like this."
"Watch me kick the ball to the wall."
"When the rope comes over, jump like this."

Feedback

There are different types of feedback that parents, coaches, and peer assistants can use as the child is practicing or performing a skill.

Positive General Feedback

This is a supportive statement about the child's motor skill response that is general in nature but does not contain any specific information about the skill or performance. General comments are useful to help motivate the child to continue practicing or performing a skill but do not really have instructional value.

Examples:

"Very good!"
"Great throw"
"Nice kick"
"Great job"

Positive Specific Feedback

A supportive statement that includes exact information about what was good about the motor skill response. Specific positive comments are beneficial

because they help the child understand exactly what part of their skill performance was correct.

Examples:

"Good, you kept your feet straight!"
"Aaron, I like the way you stepped forward when swinging the bat."
"Excellent job Mark, stepping with your opposite foot when you throw the ball."
"That's the way to bend your knees when you jump."
"George, I like the way you used your hands to catch the ball."
"Nice strike, you kept your elbows up."

PHYSICAL ASSISTANCE

Physical assistance is used to help the student if he or she is unable to do
the activity after you have given a verbal cue and model. Children with disabilities often have disrupted sensory feedback. Disrupted sensory feedback
means that the child is not able to organize and use information from their
sensory systems effectively.

Some children cannot tolerate touch and yet other children need physical
assistance to understand what the movement should feel like. Using physical
prompts can be very beneficial for children who have poor awareness of
how to move their bodies. Parents, coaches, and peer assistants should only
physically assist the student by directing his or her body part with your hands.

For children who experience disrupted sensory feedback from their bodies,
using a touch prompt or physical assistance is more effective when combined
with a verbal cue. Based on how much support the child needs, there are three
levels of physical prompts that parents and coaches can use.

- Light—gently tap or touch the body part to be moved. This can be a light
  reminder of the position of where the body part should be or when to initi-
  ate movement. For example, a light tap on one shoulder reminds the child
  to turn their body and step with the opposite foot to throw.
- Moderate—use the hand to lightly guide body part through a movement or
  part of a movement. For example, guiding the elbow up and back to prompt
  the correct position for throwing.
- Heavy—physically assist with the movement. For example, standing
  behind the student and physically assisting them with the arm motion of
  a throw.

Here are two scenarios using various types of feedback:

Scenario 1

Tutor: Cue: "George, strike the ball."

Student: Acceptable response

Assistant: Positive Specific Reinforcement:

"Good job striking the ball, you made it over the net."

Scenario 2

Tutor: Cue: "Mark, throw the ball."

Student: Unacceptable response

Tutor: Positive General Feedback: "Good try."

Tutor: Repeat Cue and Model: "Mark, throw the ball like this."

Student: Unacceptable response

Assistant: Light physical Assistance: Taps appropriate leg and says "Step forward with this foot."

Student: Acceptable response

Assistant: Positive Specific Reinforcement:

"Nice job, I like the way you stepped when you threw the ball."

Adapted from Lieberman. L.J., & Houston-Wilson, C. (2002). *Strategies for Inclusion: Handbook for Physical Educators.* Champaign, IL: Human Kinetics.

In order to help them play, children with disabilities may need a change in some rules for playing the game, modifications in equipment, adaptations of movements or skills, or altering the environment.

The following are general suggestions that can be applied to a variety of sports or activities. Finding the modifications that work the best will vary depending on the child's abilities and needs specific to the sport or activity. What may work for one activity may not work for another. As with many things, the process is trial and error. If one thing doesn't work, try another!

Rules

A rule can be changed to allow the child with a disability to be successful.

✓ Allow extra time to move—down the court or field or between bases.
✓ Include safe zone or rest spots—providing a few rest spots next to the court or field can really help those children who have asthma or those who will fatigue easily.

✓ Substitute Movements—allow child to strike ball with their hand instead of using a bat or racquet or bounce, and catch ball instead of dribbling.

Equipment

Standard gymnasium equipment can be replaced with a variety of other objects that vary in shape, color, size, etc., that will assist your child in being able to play. General ideas include:

✓ Use larger objects (playground or beach ball). Larger balls travel slower and are easier to see when catching, striking, or kicking.
✓ Use lighter objects or balls for throwing—such as foam balls or Frisbees.
✓ Use neon/bright-colored balls or objects. Bright colors tend to (a) attract attention of children who display ADD and (b) provide better visual discrimination for children with low vision.
✓ Use a batting tee or bean bag—stationary objects are easier to hit than moving ones. Using a batting tee allows a child greater success with striking or placing a soccer ball on a bean bag.
✓ Use lightweight racquets, bats, and clubs with larger grip and strike surface. Lighter implements are easier to swing and a larger strike surface such as a plastic bat with a large head or hockey stick with a larger blade makes it easier to make contact.
✓ Make the target, goal or basket, larger—making the goal larger makes it easier to hit the target or make the goal.
✓ Lower the basket or net for a wheelchair user or child with limited gross motor skills.
✓ Use a beeper or bell ball.
✓ Use a ramp to roll ball.
✓ Use a lap doughnut to keep ball on lap.
✓ Use Velcro baseballs and catching mitts.

Modifying Exercise/Movement

Changes in the way children move or accomplish a skill may be made according to their unique needs.

✓ Use a partner for physical assistance.
✓ Allow child to use a chair or railing for balance support.
✓ Allow child to push or strike ball with hand.
✓ Allow a sibling or a friend who could assist the child to perform the skill.
✓ Allow the child to walk or run.
✓ Allow wheelchair users to hold ball in their lap during periods of movement.

✓ If child has limited strength/coordination, they can hit/push ball off of tray. A teammate can then throw, kick, or strike the ball.
✓ If child has more control of legs, replace throwing/striking with kicking a larger ball.
✓ Allow the child to roll ball instead of throwing.
✓ Allow the use of two hands instead of one for rolling, throwing, or catching ball.
✓ Allow alternative ways of throwing (e.g., sidearm or underhand).
✓ Substitute each locomotor skill with a less complex task such as a step and a two-foot jump for a gallop or a wheelchair push then a wheelchair push-up for a leap.

Environment

Safety should be a consideration when looking at the environment in which your child will be working in. However, in addition to making sure that the playing area is free of any obstacles that could be a safety hazard, there are several things that you can do to enhance the play environment.

✓ Change the size or dimensions of the playing area (field or court). Make the area of play smaller—sometimes too much space can be overwhelming to process or physically too demanding. Reduce the play area with cones or mats to create a smaller space.
✓ Shorten the length of base paths or reduce the distance to goal.
✓ Decrease the distance ball is pitched or rolled.
✓ Reduce the number of players in the game or activity.
✓ Use brightly colored tape to clearly mark the court, play area, boundaries, start line, shooting area, etc.
✓ Use bright-colored pinnies to identify teammates and opponents.
✓ Use music, a beeper ball, or auditory localizer to identify end zone, goal, or basket.
✓ Use verbal or other cues (clapping, calling, waving a flashlight) to guide correct direction of throw, kick, or travel.

MODIFYING SPORTS

Many modifications that are used by teachers in physical education to help a child find success can also be used by parents and siblings at home or by community coaches. Modifications can be made in the form of equipment, movement, rules, the number of players involved, and/or the playing area (Block, 2007; Lieberman & Houston-Wilson, 2002).

Modifications are not specific to one sport and may be used in a variety of sports. For example, in sports involving balls, your child may have more success by using a soft, slow-moving ball. The intent is to practice with your child so that they will become proficient at using the softer ball and then be able to progress to a more traditional ball.

Of course, all of the modifications listed do not need to be used. It depends on the child's abilities and needs. As with many things, the process of finding the best modification is trial and error. If one thing doesn't work, try another! There may also be modifications or variations of modifications that you, a sibling, or the coach can create without outside help!

Appendix A provides modifications and adaptations for a variety of sports that children may participate in:

Basketball	Karate	Soccer
Bowling	Lacrosse	Swimming
Football	Softball/Baseball	Volleyball/Tennis

Each sport chart provides specific modifications organized by general disability categories. Complete descriptions of these categories can be found in Appendix B.

- Autism Spectrum Disorder
- Behavior Disorders
- Communication and Understanding
- Limited mobility and gross motor skills (such as cerebral palsy, spina bifida, muscular dystrophy)
- Hearing impairments
- Visual impairments

SIBLINGS AND FRIENDS AS PEER ASSISTANTS

Today, more than ever, children with disabilities are being included with their nondisabled peers in recreational after-school and community programs. The concept of inclusion of children with disabilities has become standard practice in many school districts across the United States.

The true essence of inclusion is based on the premise that all individuals with disabilities have a right to be included in naturally occurring settings and activities with their nondisabled peers, siblings, and friends (Erwin, 1993).

In physical education classes, oftentimes, children with disabilities are provided with a peer assistant to help facilitate and reinforce instruction given by the teacher. This level of assistance found in schools today can also be carried over to the home and community by having a sibling or a friend take on the role of the peer assistant for the child with a disability.

BENEFITS

A sibling or a friend as a peer assistant can be a valuable asset in providing support and attention to the child with a disability (Block, 2007; Hodge et al., 2012; Lieberman & Houston-Wilson, 2009). The sibling relationship is often the longest and most influential of any personal relationship.

Oftentimes, parents have to spend a great deal of extra time attending to the unique needs of a child with disability. As a result, a sibling relationship is sometimes overlooked as *a contributing member* in the well-being of the child with disability (Strohm, 2002). In addition to offering much-needed support a sibling that is a peer assistant can develop many positive attributes such as tolerance and compassion, insight and maturity, as well as becoming more resilient in dealing with disability experiences, and taking pride in their brother's or sister's achievements.

Using the child's friends as peer assistants can be an effective way to provide assistance to a child with a disability in sports, fitness, and motor skill development during school, or when participating in after-school or community-based programs. Having a friend as a peer assistant can help build upon and strengthen the friendship bond, which can promote a positive impact on their relationship.

Having a sibling or a friend take part in a supportive role can prove to be a gratifying and worthwhile cause for everyone. Peer assistants can help provide one-on-one attention, guided practice, and immediate feedback, which in turn assists the child in skill development and creating important opportunities to develop social skills.

Siblings or friends can learn from each other and enjoy each other's company. They gain companionship and support and learn valuable lessons in how to give and take. Siblings and friends help teach each other social skills and play an important part in each other's identity development.

Real Life Example—Inclusion in an After-school Program

Ellie, a middle school student with a moderate cognitive disability, participates in a general physical education class with her age-appropriate peers. Ellie looks forward to time with her friends in PE class and always tries her best to keep up with her classmates.

On occasion, Ellie encounters difficulty with understanding the basic game rules and depends on her friend, Brenda, to keep her on task. Ellie is fortunate that her friend, Brenda, offers her assistance, especially when they participate in organized games.

Ellie has expressed an interest in playing on the basketball team at the local recreation and parks center. However, Ellie's mom, Jill, discouraged Ellie from participating for fear she will not be able to keep up with the other teammates and be excluded from participating. However, her friend Brenda has expressed an interest in trying out for the basketball team and suggested that they go together to the first basketball tryout practice.

Brenda introduced herself and Ellie to the head coach and explained how she would like to assist Ellie in basketball practice in order for Ellie to keep up with the rest of the team. Brenda suggested that she could play alongside Ellie as a peer assistant in practice and at basketball games.

After careful consideration, the coach decided to include both girls on the team, realizing the many benefits of this inclusive experience. With minor modification and accommodation to the basketball game, both Ellie and Brenda were able to successfully participate alongside their teammates on the local recreation and parks basketball team.

PEER ASSISTANT TRAINING

It is important to understand that using friends or siblings as peer assistants is not simply a matter of making them the partner of the child with disability and asking them to help. It requires training. When making the decision to use peer assistants, parents and coaches should first consider seeking the assistance of school personnel in training tips, communication, and basic teaching strategies.

A general physical educator that teaches inclusion classes or adapted physical educator that oversees physical education programs in the school or for the school district may be an excellent resource in providing training to the peer assistants' roles and responsibilities. (Kessler & Lytle, 2005).

Providing a peer assistant training program involves several steps, including communication techniques, instructional techniques, checking for understanding, monitoring progress and how to use behavior plans that are in place for the child with the disability (Lieberman & Houston-Wilson, 2002).

TIPS FOR PARTICIPATING ON COMMUNITY SPORT TEAMS

Before Play Begins

Before you register your child on a sport team, careful preparation is necessary to develop a positive experience not only for the child, but also for the coach and other players. The child must feel accepted as a part of the group or team and the coach must have a positive attitude and feel comfortable.

When trying to determine if a program will fit the child's needs, the first step is to ask important questions about the structure and design of the program. Parents should ask the organizers to explain various aspects of the program, including philosophy, amount of structure, supervision and resources, makeup of the teams, skill level required, expectations of participating children, policies regarding behavior, flexibility in addressing individual needs and one-on-one assistance (Coyne & Fullerton, 2014).

Once a program has been selected, the next step in working toward a successful experience for a child with a disability is to establish a proactive relationship and good communication between the parent and the coach.

- **Contact the Coach**—Contacting the coach prior to the first practice is extremely important in setting the stage for success. Surprising a coach who is not expecting the child can lead to failure before any type of physical activity begins. If possible, the coach could meet the child before the actual practice to help prepare both the coach and the child.
- **Provide Awareness**—Provide the coach with an awareness regarding their child's disability along with their abilities. Parents need to help the coach learn about the disability and provide relevant information specifically related to their child. One way a parent can help the coach learn what to expect and how best to support their child is to provide an "at a glance" information sheet (Coyne & Fullerton, 2014, p. 55).

  Information on this sheet could include describing characteristics of the disability, medical issues that may affect participation, sensory issues, best way to communicate (speaking and listening), and needs during breaks and playing time, frequently seen behaviors and possible ways to handle those behaviors.
- **Prepare the Team**—Providing an awareness of a child with a disability in a sensitive, deliberate, and matter-of-fact way can foster understanding and acceptance for the other members of a team (Lieberman & Houston-Wilson, 2002).
- **Establish Positive Rapport**—A positive rapport between the coach and the parent can greatly contribute to the success of the child in a sport/recreation program. Offer to share and discuss strategies provided in this book with the coach. The following adaptations and modifications are examples of strategies that have been used in physical education programs with success; however, they are not all-inclusive. Many times the coach or other players contribute ideas that can help the child be successful in the activity.

SUMMARY

In the United States, there are over six million people who have special health, developmental, and mental health concerns. There are multiple benefits for children with disabilities when given opportunities to participate in after-school and community recreational programs. These benefits are not limited to the participant themselves, but everyone involved can also benefit.

Parents, coaches, siblings, friends, and teammates are also provided with the opportunities to develop meaningful relationships and help a child with a disability to be involved in school and community programs. It is the intent for these experiences to lead into adulthood that will contribute to the child's overall wellness and promote a lifetime of physical activity.

Including a child into a program with typical peers needs to be a careful, thoughtful, and flexible process. With the right guidance, parents can seek out activities and advocate for their child that will result in positive experiences in physical activity programs. With the assistance of school personnel, there are many instructional strategies, modifications, and adaptations used in physical education that can help a child with a disability enjoy participating in after-school and community programs.

Modification that can help a child participate with their peers include changing the rules, equipment, the exercise or movement, and environment. Along with modifying the activity, using siblings or friends as peer assistants has many benefits for all involved.

In addition to providing one-on-one attention and immediate feedback, assisting with skill development and creating important opportunities to develop social skills, siblings and friends can learn to develop patience, empathy, dependability, pride, loyalty, and caring for a child with a disability, which will benefit them significantly throughout life with most any situation encountered.

REFERENCES

Alexander, M. & Schwager, S. (2012). *Meeting the Physical Education Needs of Children with Autism Spectrum Disorder*. Reston, VA: National Association for Sport and Physical Education.

Block, M. (2007). *A Teaching Guide to Including Children with Disabilities in General Physical Education* (3rd ed). Baltimore, MD: Paul H. Brooks.

Coyne, P. & Fullerton, A. (2014). *Supporting Individuals with Autism Spectrum Disorder*. Urbana, IL: Sagamore, 45–55, 99.

Erwin, E. J. (1993, Winter). *The Philosophy and Status of Inclusion. Envision: A Publication of the Lighthouse National Center for Vision and Child Development*. 1, 3–4.

Hodge, S., Lieberman, L., & Murata, N. (2012). *Essentials of Teaching Physical Education: Culture, Diversity, and Inclusion*. Scottsdale, AZ: Holcomb Hathaway.

Kasser, S. L., & Lytle, R. K. (2005). *Inclusive Physical Activity: A Lifetime of Opportunities*. Champaign, IL: Human Kinetics.

Lieberman, L. J., (2007). *Paraeducators in Physical Education: A Training Guide to Roles and Responsibilities*. Champaign. IL: Human Kinetics.

Lieberman, L.J., & Houston-Wilson, C. (2009). *Strategies for Inclusion: A Handbook for Physical Educators* (2nd ed). Champaign. IL: Human Kinetics.

Maheady, L. (2001). Peer-mediated instruction and interventions and children with mild disabilities. *Remedial & Special Education*, 22(1): 4–15.

Reichman, N. E., Corman, H., & Noonan, K. (2008). Impact of child disability on the family disclosures maternal. *Child Health J*, 12(6): 679–683.

Strohm, K. (2002). Siblings of children with special needs Information Sheet 22—Learning Links—Helping Kids Learn. Retrieved from: www.learninglinks.org.au.

Modifications Charts

Basketball

Mobility and Limited Gross Motor Skills	Autism Spectrum Disorder, Communication, and Understanding	Sensory—Visual	Sensory—Hearing	Behavior Disorder
Reduce number of players in the game (2 v. 2 in place of 3 on 3 basketball game)	Reduce number of players in the game (2 v. 2 in place of 3 on 3 basketball game)	Determine which color is the most visible to the student	Establish visual starting and stopping signals in place of whistle such as flicking the lights or waving a flashlight or wave red, yellow, green cards	Reduce number of players in the game (2 v. 2 in place of 3 v. 3 or 5 v. 5 basketball game)
Allow the child to travel court with ball on lap	Use picture schedules to indicate series of tasks in the game	Allow the child to feel the shape/ size of basketball used in the activity prior to play		Increase the size of the court to allow the student more personal space and less likelihood of contact
Use a lap doughnut to keep ball on lap	Review rules and expectations directly before activity occurs	Provide a tour of the court and surrounding area	Use basic hand signals/ sign for run, pass, taking turns etc.	Apply a no block or interference rule
Allow a double dribble or bounce and catch	Use demonstration to provide more visual information of skill/activity desired before and after giving verbal directions	Use bright-colored and/or larger balls for better visibility and discrimination	Teammates can use shoulder taps to indicate a whistle blown	Allow the student to choose teammates he or she is comfortable playing with or allow him or her to assist in the selection process
Use two hands instead of one to dribble the ball		Use bright-colored pinnies to identify partner, teammates, or opponents	Select the court environment with the least noise	Review rules and expectations directly before activity occurs
Include a safe zone or rest spot	Use partners, peers use cues to guide correct direction of pass or where to move on court	Widen and/or add bright colors to court markings	Only have one game at a time to eliminate noise confusion	Reduce the total time of the activity/game
Give option to shoot at a lowered and/larger basket		Use colored cones to mark corners of boundaries	Use alternative communication method if utilized by the student, (i.e., interpreter, picture board, flash cards, etc.)	
Allow the child to push ball off of tray or bowling ramp to pass ball	Use a softer ball such as Nerf ball	Use bright-colored/neon tape on backboard to identify basket	Use a small whiteboard to draw out plays	
Use a larger and/or softer ball such as a playground ball or beach ball	Place a poly spot or tape of where child is to start play	Use a beeper ball or a localizer to identify basket location		
Use a tactile or textured ball	Color code/clearly mark basket the child's team is shooting for	Use a bell basketball		
Allow the child to walk or run in a smaller court or area of play		Use a larger basket		
Use partners, peers to assist the child to dribble or pass ball	Keep sentences short, 2 to 3 words. "Stand here," "Bounce ball to…"	Use auditory start/stop signals such as music or a whistle		
Use partners, peers to pick up ball and put on the child's tray or lap		Use enlarged illustrations of correct skill/task (e.g., bounce pass)		

Adapted from Block, (2007); Lieberman. L.J., & Houston-Wilson, C., (2002).

Bowling

Mobility and Limited Gross Motor Skills	Autism Spectrum Disorder, Communication, and Understanding	Sensory—Visual	Sensory—Hearing	Behavior Disorder
Use two hands instead of one to roll the ball Use bumpers and/or bowling ramp Use a smaller ball Use a lighter or rubber bowling ball Use a bowling ball with a retractable handle Reduce the number of steps prior to rolling the ball Allow the child to sit in chair stand with hand on the back of a chair for stability Allow the child to remain in a stationary position when rolling the ball Use bumpers to keep the ball in play Use a partner for physical assistance Use bumpers and/or bowling ramp	Place a poly spot or tape of where the child is to start to start roll/3 step approach Use bright-colored or wider paint/tape to mark start line, arrows on lane and lane markings Use picture schedules to show the sequence of tasks Enlarge illustrations to give a visual cue of the skill Review rules and expectations directly before activity occurs Use demonstrations to provide more visual information of skill/activity desired before and after giving verbal directions Use partners, peers use cues to guide correct direction of where to roll ball	Use bright-colored or wider paint/tape to mark start line, arrows on lane and lane markings Use a neon or bright-colored bowling ball Use a bowling ramp Use partners, peers use cues to guide correct direction of where to roll ball Use verbal cues or other cues (clapping, calling, wave a flashlight) to guide direction of travel Enlarge illustrations of the skill for those with low vision Orient the child to seating area, ball return, scoring stand and walk lane prior to play Allow the child to feel the shape/size of bowling ball and ball return Give continuous verbal cues	Use neon tape to mark start line, arrows on lane and lane markings for better discrimination Establish visual starting and stopping signals such as waving a flashlight or wave red, yellow, green cards Post illustrations of the 3 step approach Use visual start and stop signals or taking turns such as flicking the lights, waving a flag, hand or flashlight Implement a hand signal that the child understands for run, stop	Create space between lanes—place players in every other lane to reduce proximity Decrease the number of players on each lane to reduce the chance of physical contact Allow students to choose someone they are comfortable playing with or allow them to assist in selection process Provide a cool down/time-out area to allow the student to gain self-control Post and review rules and expectations for behavior directly before activity occurs

Adapted from Block, (2007); Lieberman. L.J., & Houston-Wilson, C., (2002).

Dance-Creative Movement

Mobility and Limited Gross Motor Skills	Autism Spectrum Disorder, Communication, and Understanding	Sensory—Visual	Sensory—Hearing	Behavior Disorder
Use supports such as chairs, or step ladders in choreography	Provide the same structure for each class	Provide tactile assistance for body positioning—allow the child to "feel" the body alignment and movement as the teacher performs it	Use basic hand signals/sign language to communicate	Begin class with opportunities to reinforce self-esteem or express feelings
Use slow tempo music	Concrete cues	Physically assist the child to perform the movement	Establish visual starting and stopping signals such as flicking the lights or waving a flashlight or hand	Allow the student to choose music
Decrease the distance to travel when designing choreography	Utilize pictures or symbols	Have students hold hands when traveling throughout the room	Use bright-colored markers on floor to indicate path, direction, or pattern of movement	Designate specific space or area to go when needing a break or time out
Utilize partners to assist movement	Decrease volume level of music for children who are sound sensitive	Be specific when giving directions of body movements	Establish and give a sign count for each step similar to a verbal count for hearing dancers	Provide opportunities for relaxation
Decrease the number of movements in the dance	Consider using earplugs or headphones	Use peer to help provide direction	Allow the child to feel the music source, speaker. (Many deaf dancers can discriminate bass tones better than treble tones.)	Use breathing techniques for calming
Allow alternative movements for performing dance movement/step	Decrease the number of movements in the dance	Be consistent in language—use the same words the same words for choreography	You/they clap the timing with the hands so performer can see and feel tempo/rhythm of the dance step	
Substitute arm movements for steps or leg movements	Use peer to assist in providing direction	Use bright-colored markers on floor to indicate path, direction or pattern of movement	Use a small whiteboard to draw out dance pattern	
	Use colored markers on floor to indicate path, direction or pattern of movement	Provide specific counts to move on	Use picture schedules to indicate series of steps in the dance	
		Clap the rhythm with their hands		
		Have dance partners wear bells on waist, or wrist		
		Have dance partners wear a neon/ bright pinnie		

Adapted from Block, (2007); Lieberman. L.J., & Houston-Wilson, C., (2002).

Football (Flag)

Mobility and Limited Gross Motor Skills

- Use a smaller and/or softer ball such as a Nerf ball
- Use Velcro balls and catching mitts
- Shorten the distance ball is tossed or toss ball underhand rather than throwing overhand
- Hand off ball rather than pass
- Allow alternative ways of throwing (e.g., sidearm, underhand) or substitute rolling the ball for throwing
- Allow extra time to pass or receive a pass
- Use longer or shorter flags
- Use only one flag

Autism Spectrum Disorder, Communication and Understanding

- Expand or reduce the time in the task
- Use uniforms or pinnies to identify teammates and opponents
- Use pictures/illustrations of correct skill performance
- Use picture schedules to indicate series of tasks in the game (e.g., hike, run pass, catch run)
- Review rules and expectations directly before activity occurs
- Use picture cards with rule infractions
- Have partners use cues to guide correct direction of throw or where to run
- Use a softer ball such as Nerf ball
- Place a poly spot or tape of where the child is to stand and run/move to (base)
- Keep sentences short, 2 to 3 words. "Stand here," "Run to right," "Look for pass"

Sensory—Visual

- Allow the child to feel the shape/size of equipment used in the activity prior to play for tactile information
- Use auditory start/stop signals such as a whistle
- Allow the child to feel the shape/size of equipment used in the activity prior to play for tactile information
- Use colored cones to mark corners of boundaries
- Use verbal cues or other cues (clapping, calling, wave a flashlight) to guide correct direction of throw or travel
- Use partners, peers to cue correct direction of throw or where to run/move
- Use neon or bright-colored pinnies to identify partner, teammates, or opponents

Sensory—Hearing

- Establish visual starting and stopping signals such as flicking the lights or using a flashlight along with the use of red, yellow, green cards
- Use hand or flag to signal start and stop play
- Have all players raise their hand when a whistle is blown to stop play
- Use cards with rule infractions
- Identify, then eliminate, excessive noise to help reduce noise confusion
- Use neon or bright-colored Football
- Use neon or bright-colored pinnies to identify partner, teammates, or opponents
- Use bright-colored or wider paint or tape to identify field markings for better visibility and discrimination
- Use colored cones to mark corners of boundaries/ corners

Behavior Disorder

- Review rules and expectations directly before activity occurs
- Designate a specific area or person to go to if the child needs a calming break during game play
- Reduce number of participants in task or increase size of playing field to allow the student more personal space and less likelihood of contact
- Allow the student to choose teammates he or she is comfortable playing with or allow him or her to assist in the selection process
- Review rules and expectations directly before activity occurs
- Give additional points for good sportsmanship
- Reduce the total time of the activity/game

Karate (Martial Arts)

Mobility and Limited Gross Motor Skills	Autism Spectrum Disorder, Communication, and Understanding	Sensory—Visual	Sensory—Hearing	Behavior Disorder
Provide support when balance is challenged (a chair, the wall)	Use mirrors	Provide tactile assistance for body positioning—allow the child to "feel" the initial position and movement as the teacher performs it	Use sign language or hand signs	No contact
Give additional time for movement	Provide pictures of movements	Talk through the steps	Use neon tape to mark strike zone on pad	Designate personal space
Use only upper movements body for children in wheelchairs	Provide written routine and schedule of class (bow, etc.)	Use neon tape to mark strike zone on pad	Use basic hand signals/sign language to communicate	No kicks below belt
Substitute arm movements for steps or leg movements	Attach to a punching pad, a memory foam pillow cut into square punching targets with an ink imprint of the correct position for punching, have the child attempt to punch over to make the impression look the same	Be consistent in language for directions	Establish visual starting and stopping signals such as flicking the lights or waving a flashlight or hand	Provide opportunities for relaxation. Use breathing techniques for calming
Allow alternative movements for performing step	Use peer to assist in providing direction	Use peer to help provide direction	Use bright-colored markers on floor to indicate path, direction, or pattern of movement	Have set rules and consequences established between the parents, the instructor and the child
Attach to a punching pad a memory foam pillow cut into square punching targets with an ink imprint of the correct position for punching, and have the child attempt to punch over to make the impression look the same	Use colored markers on floor to indicate path, direction, or pattern of movement	Use bright-colored markers on floor to indicate path, direction, or pattern of movement	Establish and give a sign count for each step similar to a verbal count for hearing partners	Designate a specific area and possibly a time frame to go for a "time out" before returning to activity
Utilize partners to assist movement		Provide specific counts to move on	You/they clap the timing with the hands so performer can see and feel tempo/rhythm of the movement	
Decrease the number of movements in the sequence		Have sparring partners wear bells on waist or wrist	Use a small whiteboard to draw out movement pattern	
			Use picture schedules to indicate series of steps in the dance	

Lacrosse

Mobility and Limited Gross Motor Skills	Autism Spectrum Disorder, Communication, and Understanding	Sensory—Visual	Sensory—Hearing	Behavior Disorder
Include a safe zone or rest spot	Reduce number of participants in task	Allow the child to feel the shape/size of equipment used in the activity prior to play for tactile information	Establish visual starting and stopping signals in place of whistle such as flicking the lights or waving a flashlight or wave red, yellow, green cards	Reduce the number of participants in task or increase the size of playing field to allow the student more personal space and less likelihood of contact
Give option to shoot at an open goal	Include a safe zone or rest spot	Use a bright-colored and/or wide paint to identify baseline and field markings	Use basic hand signals/sign for run, pass, taking turns etc.	Include a safe zone or rest spot
Use a softer ball such as a tennis or rubber ball	Expand or reduce the time in the task	Use a bright-colored ball	Teammates can use shoulder taps to indicate a whistle blown	Allow the student to choose teammates he or she is comfortable playing with or allow him or her to assist in the selection process
Tie strap shortened stick to wheelchair	Use pinnies to identify teammates and opponents	Use bright-colored pinnies to identify teammates and/or opponents	Use hand or flag to signal start and stop play	Review rules and expectations directly before activity occurs
Strap hand to a shortened stick for wheelchair user with limited grip strength	Use pictures/illustrations of correct skill performance	Use a localizer to identify goal location	Have all players hold sticks up when whistle is blown to stop play	
Allow the child to walk or run in a smaller area of play	Use picture schedules to indicate series of tasks in the game (e.g., scoop ball cradle, pass)	Have partners use cues to guide correct direction of throw or where to run	Only have one game at a time to eliminate noise confusion	
Allow wheelchair user to hold ball in lap	Review rules and expectations directly before activity occurs	Use auditory start/stop signals with a whistle	Use alternative communication method if utilized by the student, (i.e., interpreter, picture board, flash cards, etc.)	
	Have partners use cues to guide correct direction of throw or where to run	Use partners, peers to cue correct direction of throw or where to run/move	Use a small whiteboard to draw out plays	

Adapted from Block, (2007); Lieberman. L.J., & Houston-Wilson, C., (2002).

Mobility and Limited Gross Motor Skills	Autism Spectrum Disorder, Communication and Understanding	Sensory - Visual	Sensory - Hearing	Behavior Disorder
Substitute rolling the ball for kicking	Place a poly spot or tape of where the child is to start play	Shorten the distance between partners or to goal	Use hand or flag to signal start and stop play	Reduce number of players in the game
Allow the child to walk or run in a smaller area of play	Color code/clearly mark goal that the child's team is shooting for	Use partners, peers use cues to guide correct direction of kick or where to run	Establish visual starting and stopping signals such as flicking the	Increase size of the play area to allow the student
If wheelchair user allow the child to hit/push ball off of lap or tray, the peer then kicks ball	Use picture schedules to indicate series of tasks in the game	Use a bell or beeper soccer ball	lights or waving a flashlight or wave	more personal space and less likelihood of
	Use colored cones to mark corners of boundaries/corners	Use neon or bright-colored Soccer ball	red, yellow, green cards	contact
Allow alternative ways of kicking such as use a *bowling ramp* to pass ball	Use, neon/ bright-colored balls and/or larger for better visibility and discrimination	Use a lager/softer ball such as a beach ball, tactile ball, or Nerf ball	Implement a hand signal that child	Apply a no block or interference rule
Use a larger and/or softer ball such as a Nerf ball	Use a slightly deflated ball	Use a slightly deflated ball	understands for run, stop, taking turns	Allow the student to choose
Shorten the distance between partners or to goal	Review rules and expectations directly before activity occurs	Enlarge and laminate illustrations to give a visual cue of the task	Use neon or bright-colored Soccer ball	teammates he or she is comfortable
	Keep sentences short, 2 to 3 words "Stand here," "Kick ball"	Use auditory start/stop signals such as a whistle	Use neon or bright-colored pinnies to	playing with or allow him or her
Allow the child to kick a stationary ball placed on a bean bag	Use demonstrations to provide more visual information of skill/ activity desired before and after giving verbal directions	Allow child to feel the shape/size of equipment and prior to play for tactile information	identify partner, teammates or opponents	to assist in the selection process
Use partners, peers to assist the child to kick	Pictures are helpful to use because children primarily process information visually	Orient child to size of play area and location of goals prior to play	Use brightly colored or wider paint or tape to identify	Review rules and expectations directly before
If the child has more control of arms, replace kicking with throwing/ a smaller ball	Place a poly spot or tape of where the child is to stand and run/ move to	Use brightly colored or wider paint or tape to identify field markings for better visibility and discrimination	court markings for better visibility and discrimination	activity occurs
Use a slightly deflated ball	Use picture symbols for prompting of skill, hold a picture of someone kicking to prompt the child to kick	Use neon or bright-colored pinnies to identify partner, teammates or opponents	Use colored cones to mark corners of boundaries/corners	Reduce the total time of the activity/game
		Use colored cones to mark corners of boundaries/corners		
		Use verbal cues or other cues (clapping, calling, wave a flashlight) to guide correct direction of throw or travel		
		Assign a peer to signal child on directions, skills, etc.		

Adapted from Block, (2007); Lieberman. L.J., & Houston-Wilson, C., (2002).

Softball/Baseball

Mobility and Limited Gross Motor Skills	Autism Spectrum Disorder, Communication, and Understanding	Sensory—Visual	Sensory—Hearing	Behavior Disorder
Use a larger and/or softer ball that track slower (e.g., balloon, playground ball, volleyball trainer, beach ball, tactile ball)	Reduce number of participants in task	Use a bright-colored and/or wide paint to identify baseline and field markings	Use hand or flag to signal start and stop play	Reduce number of participants in task or increase size of playing field to allow the student more personal space and less likelihood of contact
Use Velcro baseballs and catching mitts	Expand or reduce the time in the task	Use colored cones to mark bases and/or boundaries	Have a teammate wave to stop in play	Allow the student to choose teammates he or she is comfortable playing with or allow him or her to assist in the selection process
Use a batting tee to push or hit the ball	Use pinnies to identify teammates and opponents	Use a bright-colored ball	Identify, then eliminate, excessive noise to help reduce noise confusion	Review rules and expectations directly before activity occurs
Use a lighter bat (plastic) and/or larger bat	Use pictures/illustrations of correct skill performance	Allow the child to use batting tee	Use neon or bright-colored pinnies to identify partner, teammates or opponents	
Shorten the distance the ball is tossed or pitched when trying to hit a baseball or softball	Use picture symbols for prompting of skill, hold a picture of someone striking to prompt the child to swing	Use a beeper ball to identify pitch location	Establish visual starting and stopping signals such as waving a hand or flashlight	
Shorten the distance between players or to base	Use picture schedules to indicate series of tasks in the game (e.g., hit ball, run to 1st base)	Use a beeper localizer to identify base location		
Allow extra time to move between bases	Use poly spots with numbers if there is a specific sequence - (e.g., 1st, 2nd, 3rd, base)	Use spotters in the outfield to identify ball direction and location		
Toss ball underhand rather than throw overhand	Review rules and expectations directly before activity occurs	Have partners use cues to guide correct direction of throw or where to run		
Strike a ball on a string hung from a basketball rim when practicing	Have partners assist or use cues to guide correct direction of throw or where to run	Allow extra time to move between bases		
Allow alternative ways of throwing (e.g., sidearm, underhand) or substitute rolling the ball for throwing	Use a softer ball such as a yarn or Nerf ball	Use auditory start/stop signals such as a whistle		
Allow the child to hit/push ball off tray, and the peer then throws or strikes ball	Place a poly spot or tape of where the child is to stand in the outfield or run/move to (base)	Allow the child to feel the shape/size of equipment used in the activity prior to play for tactile information		
If the child has more control of legs, replace throwing/striking with kicking a larger ball	Keep sentences short, 2 to 3 words "Stand here," "Strike ball"	Orient the child to environment and play area along with the location of bases/boundaries prior to play		
Use partners, peers to assist the child to throw		Implement a hand signal that the child understands for running, stopping, or taking turns		
		Use verbal or other cues (clapping, calling, waving a flashlight) to guide correct direction of throw or travel		
		Use partners or peers to cue correct direction of throw or where to run/move		
		Use verbal cues such as "Ready, Pitch/throw" to tell the child when ball is released for catching		
		Use neon or bright-colored pinnies to identify partner, teammates, or opponents		
		Enlarge illustrations to give visual cue of the tasks		

Adapted from Block, (2007); Lieberman. L.J., & Houston-Wilson, C., (2002).

Swimming

Mobility and Limited Gross Motor Skills	Autism Spectrum Disorder, Communication, and Understanding	Sensory—Visual	Sensory—Hearing	Behavior Disorder
Consider water temperature, which should be above 80 Utilize flotation devices, such as aqua joggers, noodles, and rafts Use water shoes or socks to prevent abrasions on the feet from the bottom of the pool	Develop trust through games and water play Use pictures/illustrations/video clips of correct skill performance	Provide a tactile tour of the pool, indicating the depths of the water Use hand over hand or hand under hand instruction When swimming have someone on the deck be responsible to cue to avoid running into the side of the pool Neon/bright lane lines	Have a planned and rehearsed signal for gaining the attention of the child Have a planned emergency signal that the child understands what to do if he she observes the signal Use modeling, signs, or gestures Have a dry erase board available to write or draw pictures	Develop trust through games and water play

Volleyball/Tennis

Mobility and Limited Gross Motor Skills	Autism Spectrum Disorder, Communication, and Understanding	Sensory—Visual	Sensory—Hearing	Behavior Disorder
Use a larger and/or softer ball such as a balloon, a Nerf ball, or beach ball for volleyball	Expand or reduce the time in the task	Use a larger foam/practice tennis ball	Use hand or light signals to start and stop play	Reduce number of players in the game
Use a foam/practice tennis ball	Use different colored pinnies to differentiate teammates and opponents	Use a racquet with a bigger head	Teammate shoulder taps to stop in play	Increase size of court to allow the student more personal space and less likelihood of contact
Use a lightweight racquet and/or one with a bigger head	Use a softer ball such as a Nerf ball	Use neon/bright-colored or wider or textured tape to identify court markings	If the student uses an interpreter, make sure that the interpreter is available through the duration of the assessment	Allow the student to choose teammates he or she is comfortable playing with or allow him or her to assist in the selection process
If limited strength/coordination have the individual hit/push ball off of tray or lap	Use floor spots with numbers if there is a specific sequence (e.g., rotation on volleyball court)	Use neon/bright-colored tape to identify top of the net	Select the court environment with the least noise	Review rules and expectations directly before activity occurs
Use partners or peers to pick up ball and put on the child's tray or lap	Use picture schedules to indicate series of tasks in the game	Use neon or bright-colored ball	Only have one game to eliminate noise confusion	Reduce the total time of the activity/game
Substitute throwing the ball for striking	Keep sentences short, 2 to 3 words. "Stand here"	Use bright-colored pinnies for teammates		
Lower nets for limited gross motor skills	Use demonstrations to provide more visual information of skill/activity desired before and after giving verbal directions	Use a beeper ball and/or a localizer to identify ball location		
Remove the net—instead designate a line that the ball needs to travel over	Allow partners or peers to use cues to guide correct direction of striking ball or where to stand	Select the court environment with the least noise		
Reduce the distance for serving		Only have one game to eliminate noise confusion		
Allow to serve ball using a batting tee		Allow partners or peers to use cues to guide correct direction of striking ball or where to stand/move		
Allow two steps or unlimited steps for serving		Use auditory start/stop signals such as music or a whistle		
		Allow the child to feel the shape/size of equipment used in the activity prior to play for tactile information		

(Continued)

Volleyball/Tennis (*Continued*)

Allow the student to strike or catch ball after one or two bounces	Use pictures of skill performance because children primarily process information visually	Use larger, neon or bright-colored balls or balloons for better visibility and discrimination (e.g., playground ball, volleyball trainer, beach ball, tactile ball) and track slower	Allow the alternative communication method (i.e., interpreter, picture board, flash cards, etc.) utilized by the player
Reduce the number of participants in the task	Enlarge and laminate illustrations to give a visual cue of the task	Use a bell or beeper volleyball	
If grip is weak, use ace bandage or Velcro strip to anchor hand to racquet handle	Place a poly spot or tape to stand for different positions on the volleyball court	Use bright-colored or wider paint or tape to identify court markings for better visibility and discrimination	
Allow the child to sit in a chair or provide the back of a chair for stability if unable to stand independently or if the child has balance issues	Use picture communication symbols for prompting of skill, for example, hold a picture of someone serving to prompt the child to serve	Use colored cones to mark corners of boundaries	
Use partners, peers to guide correct movement		Use neon or bright-colored pinnies to identify partner, teammates, or opponents	
		Use verbal cues or other cues (clapping, calling, wave a flashlight) to guide correct direction of hit or travel	
		Use partners, peers to cue correct direction of throw or where to run/move	
		Establish visual starting and stopping signals such as flicking the lights or waving a flashlight or wave red, yellow, green cards	
		Use a bell or beeper ball	
		Use a batting tee for serving	
		Enlarge illustrations to give visual cue of the task	
		Implement a hand signal that the child understands for running, stopping, or taking turns	

Adapted from Block, (2007); Lieberman. L.J., & Houston-Wilson, C., 2002.

Appendix A

Adapted Sports Organizations and Resources

ADAPTED SPORTS ORGANIZATIONS

American Association of Adapted Sports Programs
http://www.adaptedsports.org

America's Athletes With Disabilities, Inc.
http://www.americasathletes.org

Athletes with Disability Network
http://www.adnpage.org

Boccia
http://www.teamusa.org

Challenged Athletes Foundation
http://www.challengedathletes.org

Disability Sports USA
http://www.disabledsportsusa.org/

Dwarf Athletic Association of America
http://www.daaa.org

General Wheelchair Sports
http://www.apparelyzed.com/support/sport/wsusa.html

Goalball: Unites States Association of Blind Athletes
http://www.usaba.org

Goalball
http://www.dhamilton.net/goalball

Inclusive Fitness Coalition
http://www.incfit.org

International Wheelchair Basketball Federation
http://www.iwbf.org

National Beep Baseball Association
http://www.nbba.org

National Sports Center for the Disabled
http://www.nscd.org

National Wheelchair Basketball Association (NWBA)
http://www.nwba.org

Sitting Volleyball: USA Volleyball Headquarters
http://www.teamusa.org/USA-Volleyball/USA-Teams/Sitting-Volleyball

Skating Association for the Blind and Handicapped, Inc. (SABAH)
http://www.sabahinc.org

Special Olympics
http://www.specialolympics.org

U.S. Aquatics Association of the Deaf
http://www.nchpad.org

Wheelchair & Ambulatory Sports, USA
http://www.wasusa.org

Wheelchair Racquetball
http://www.usra.org

Wheelchair Tennis
wheelchair@itftennis.com

World T.E.A.M. Sports
http://worldteamsports.org

U.S. Electric Wheelchair Hockey Association
http://www.usewha.org

United States Hand cycle Association
http://www.ushf.org

United States Quad Rugby Association (USA)
http://usgra.org

USA Swimming
http://www.usaswimming.org

USA Deaf Sports Federation
http://www.usdeafsports.org/

RESOURCES

American Art Therapy Association
http://www.arttherapy.org/

American Dance Therapy Association
http://www.adta.org/

American Music Therapy Association
http://www.musictherapy.org/

American Therapeutic Recreation Association
https://www.atra-online.com/

Best Buddies International (BBI)
http://www.bestbuddies.org/

Boys and Girls Club of America
http://www.bgca.org/

Council for Exceptional Children
http://www.cec.sped.org/

Lose the Training Wheels
http://icanshine.org

National Ability Center
http://www.discovernac.org

National Arts and Disability Center
http://www.semel.ucla.edu/

National Consortium for Physical Education and Recreation for Individuals with Disabilities
http://www2.gcs.k12.in.us/ldoherty/index_files/index/Web%20sites%20
for%20Adaptive%20P.E/NCPERID%20Homepage.htm

National Center on Physical Activity and Disability (NCPAD)
http://www.ncperd.org

National Dissemination Center for Children with Disabilities PACER
http://www.parentcenterhub.org/nichcy-gone/

National Recreation and Parks Association
http://nrpa.org

PATH International Professional Association of Therapeutic Horsemanship International
http://www.pathintl.org/

PACER Center—Champions for Children with Disabilities
http://www.pacer.org/

PE Central
http://www.pecentral.org

PELINKS4U—Adapted Physical Education
http://www.pelinks4u.org/covey/adapted/adapted.htm

SHAPE America
http://www.shapeamerica.org/

The National Center on Physical Activity and Disability
http://www.nchpad.org

YMCA
http://www.ymca.net/

EQUIPMENT COMPANIES

Adaptive Sports Equipment
http://www.adaptivesportsequipment.com/

Flaghouse
http://www.flaghouse.com

Discount School Supply
http://www.discountschoolsupply.com/

Gym Closet
http://www.gymcloset.com

Gopher Sport
http://www.gophersport.com

S&S Worldwide: Crafts, Games, Party, Recreation Supplies
http://www.ssww.com

Palos Sports
http://www.palossports.com

Abilitations
http://www.abilitations.com

PE Products
http://www.aph.org/pe/products.html

Freedom Concepts Inc.
http://www.freedomconcepts.com

Top End
http://www.topendwheelchair.com

Spokes'n Motion
http://www.spokesnmotion.com

PERIODICALS

Ability http://www.abilitymagazine.com/

Active Living www.activelivingmagazine.com

Adapted Physical Activity Quarterly http://www.humankinetics.com/APAQ/journalAbout.cfm

Journal of Physical Education, Recreation and Dance www.aahperd.org/aahperd/template.cfm?template=johperd_main.html

Kids on Wheels www.kidsonwheels.cc

New Mobility www.newmobility.com

Palaestra http://www.palaestra.com/

Sports and Spokes http://www.pvamagazines.com/sns/

Teaching Exceptional Children http://escholarship.bc.edu/education/tecplus/

The Exceptional Parent http://www.eparent.com/

Appendix B

General Modifications Chart

	Object Control—Kick	*Object Control—Throw/Roll*	*Object Control—Catch/Strike*
Mobility	Increase size of target or use a wider goal	Use a whiffle ball or a weighted bean bag	Use a Velcro ball and mitt
	Use a larger ball, Nerf ball or beach ball, balloons	Shorten the distance between partners or to base	Use a larger and/or softer ball such as a balloon/Nerf ball or beach ball
	Shorten the distance ball is rolled or kicked	Give option to shoot at a lowered and/larger basket	Use a lightweight racquet or clubs
	Allow the child to walk or run in a smaller area of play for soccer	Substitute rolling the ball for throwing	Use Velcro baseballs and catching mitts
	For a wheelchair user, tie a short floor hockey stick to chair to dribble or pass ball	Use two hands instead of one to roll the ball	Use a batting tee to push or hit the ball
	Use a slightly deflated ball so that it doesn't roll very far when dribbling	Reduce the number of steps prior to rolling the ball	Use a lighter bat (plastic) and/or a larger bat or an object
	Provide choice of different distances to travel, pass, or dribble	Allow the child to walk or run in a smaller area of play for basketball	Shorten the distance ball is tossed or pitched when trying to hit a baseball or softball
	Walk and dribble instead of run and dribble	Allow the child to sit in a chair or provide the back of a chair for stability if the child is unable to stand independently or has balance issues	Toss ball underhand rather than throwing overhand
	Replace selected foot skills with hand or eye movements	Use partners or peers to pick up ball and put on the child's tray or lap	Strike a ball on a string hung from tree limb or a basketball rim
	Replace dribbling by holding ball on lap and push wheelchair to travel distance while the child repeatedly hits ball	If limited strength/coordination can hit/push ball off of tray, peer then throws or strikes ball	Allow extra time to move between bases
	Peer pushes wheelchair while the child holds ball in lap or hands during periods of movement	If the child has more control of legs, replace throwing/striking with kicking a larger ball	Lower nets for tennis or volleyball limited gross motor skills
	Assist the child in moving foot to kick ball	Allow alternative ways of throwing (e.g., sidearm, underhand)	Remove the net—instead designate a line that the ball needs to travel over
	Kick ball or push ball off of foot rests	Use a bowling ramp	Allow two steps or unlimited steps for serving
	Push ball using hands down ramp, off tray or lap toward goal or another player	Substitute each locomotor skill with a less complex task such as a wheelchair push then a wheelchair push-up for skipping or a step and a two-foot jump for a gallop	Allow the student to strike ball after two or three bounces
	Give the child the option to play position that requires less mobility (e.g., goalie)		

Autism Spectrum Disorder, Communication and Understanding	Give extra demonstrations after giving verbal directions Utilize a picture schedule to help with predictability of game Give verbal/picture cue of what comes next during game/activity Place a poly spot or tape of where the child is to stand and/or dribble to Use floor spots with numbers for drills with a specific sequence Review rules and expectations directly before activity occurs Keep sentences short, two to three words. "Stand here," Kick hard, Kick past line" Add rule that no one can steal the ball when the child is dribbling or passing Place a poly spot or tape of where the child is to stand	Use picture schedules to indicate series of tasks in the game Review rules and expectations directly before activity occurs Use modeling/demonstrations to provide more visual information of skill/activity desired before and after giving verbal directions Use partners, peers use cues to guide correct direction of throw or where to run Use a softer ball such as a yarn or Nerf ball Pictures are helpful to use because children primarily process information visually Enlarge and laminate illustrations to give a visual cue of the task Place a poly spot or tape of where the child is to stand and run/move to (base)	Use floor spots with numbers if there is a specific sequence - (e.g., 1st, 2nd, 3rd, base) Keep sentences short, 2 to 3 words. "Stand here," "Strike ball" For children with limited gross motor skills follow suggestions under Mobility
Sensory—Visual	Use auditory start/stop signals such as music or a whistle Enlarge illustrations to give visual cue of the task for those who have some vision Use a bright neon ball Use a bell or beeper ball Use verbal cues to tell the child when ball is released for trapping or indicate direction of pass Use partners, peers use cues (clapping, calling, wave a flashlight) to guide correct direction of dribble or pass	Use a larger basket Use auditory start/stop signals such as music or a whistle Allow the child to feel the shape/size of equipment used in the activity prior to play for tactile information Use neon or bright-colored balls. bean bags, balloons Use a bell or beeper ball Use bright-colored or wider paint or tape to identify court markings for better visibility and discrimination	Use balloons, neon or bright-colored balls or larger (or both) for better visibility and discrimination Use larger or textured balls that track slower (e.g., playground ball, volleyball trainer, beach ball, tactile ball) Use a bell or beeper ball Use a batting T Use a bright ball on a string hung from a basketball rim

	Object Control—Kick	*Object Control—Throw/Roll*	*Object Control—Catch/Strike*
	Have teammates give extra verbal cues to the child to describe where s/he is and where teammates and opponents are Have the peer and the child hold a short length of rope, using it to guide the child dribbling Have the child dribble along wall or fence so that s/he can place hand against it for reference Place a radio behind the middle of the goal to cue the child where to shoot Place a string of lights around basket to illuminate goal Attach an object to target (e.g., bells on a string) that makes noise when hit Use neon or bright-colored tape and/or pinnies to identify teammates or other childs	Use colored cones to mark corners of boundaries Use verbal cues or other cues (clapping, calling, wave a flashlight) to guide correct direction of throw or travel Use partners, peers to cue correct direction of throw or where to run/move Use neon or bright-colored pinnies to identify partner, teammates or opponents	Use verbal cues to tell the child when ball is released for catching or indicate direction of throw Use neon or bright-colored pinnies to identify partner, teammates or opponents Use brightly colored or wider paint or tape to identify court markings for better visibility and discrimination Use colored cones to mark corners of boundaries Allow the child to strike or catch ball after one or two bounces Use brightly colored tape on top of tennis or volleyball net for better visibility and discrimination
Sensory—Hearing	Establish visual starting and stopping signals such as flicking the lights or flashlight, waving a neon scarf or flash card (red-stop, yellow-slow, green-go) Enlarge/laminate activity diagrams to allow for better understanding of directions	Establish visual starting and stopping signals such as flicking the lights or waving a flashlight or wave red, yellow, green cards Enlarge illustrations to give visual cue of the task Use picture symbols for prompting of skill, hold a picture of someone throwing to prompt the child to throw Implement a hand signal that the child understands for running, stopping, or taking turns Assign a peer to signal the child on directions, skills, etc Allow the child to use batting tee, larger hockey stick, a smaller golf club with bigger ball (beach ball)	

Index

academics performance, physical education and, 4

action plan, for community programs, 43–44; for elementary level, *45*; for high school, *45*; for middle school, *45*

active communication, 24, 26

active movement guidelines: for infants, 17; for preschoolers, 17–18; for toddlers, 17

adapted equipment, at home, 34–35

adapted physical education (APE), 1, 2, 56

Adapted Sports Organizations, 8

advocacy, of parents/guardians, 7–8, 23–25

affective learning, 3

after-school programs: community, 35, 42; extracurricular activities for, 4–5; on IEP and 504 plans, 49; law and, 46–48

American Academy of Pediatrics, 17

Americans with Disability Act, 48

APE. *See* adapted physical education

ASD. *See* Autism Spectrum Disorder

ASD, communication, and understanding modifications charts, *107*

assessment, of disabled children, *44*

assistive technology, 6–7

Autism Spectrum Disorder (ASD), 1, 53, 59–63, 71

balance, 15

barriers, hurdles and, 24–25, *25*

basketball modification charts, *88*

benefits, of peer assistants, 81

benefits, of physical education, 3, 4, 5, 7, 13, 42; instructional strategies and, 72–74, 81–82

Bloom's Taxonomy of Learning: affective, 3; cognitive, 3; psychomotor, 3

boundary modifications, 28

bowling modification charts, *89*

caregivers, as facilitators, 16–17

Centers for Disease Control (CDC) and Prevention, 4, 5, 22

central nervous system disorder, 11

Chad: with autism, 71; soccer experience of, 71–72, 73

charts. *See* modification charts

child-based modifications, 26, 27–28, 34–35

children, with disabilities. *See* disabled children

child: voice of, 35–37. *See also* early childhood development

About the Editor

Rocco Aiello works for St. Mary's County Public Schools, Maryland, as a coordinator of Adapted Physical Education and Corollary Sports through the Department of Special Education. Rocco provides educational guidance to physical education teachers and other district personnel within the twenty-seven schools in St. Mary's County. In 2008, Rocco was named the National Teacher of the Year in Adapted Physical Education.

Mr. Aiello also directs and teaches children with disabilities in the Adapted Aquatics and Camp Inspire programs offered through the Department of Recreation and Parks. He is a strong supporter of the St. Mary's County Special Olympics and Southern Maryland U.S. Paralympic Programs.

Rocco has coauthored one book chapters and has written numerous articles throughout his twenty-five-year career in physical education.

Rocco received his MS from The College at Brockport in Adapted Physical Education and his post-master's certification in Administration and Supervision from Townson University.

About the Contributors

Dr. Ronald Davis is professor of Adapted Physical Education/Activity at Texas Woman's University. He teaches in the undergraduate, masters, doctoral programs, and helps coordinate a U.S. Department of Education professional preparation grant. Dr. Davis taught for twenty years at Ball State University and helped implement three training camps for the United States Paralympics for Korea, Barcelona, and Atlanta Games. He has been in higher education for over thirty years teaching in the area of adapted physical education and disability sport. He has authored two editions of a textbook on the topic of disability sport.

Justin A. Haegele, PhD, CAPE, is an assistant professor with the Department of Human Movement Sciences at Old Dominion University. He received his doctorate at The Ohio State University in 2015 in adapted physical education. Prior to pursuing his PhD, Dr. Haegele was an adapted physical education teacher at an elementary school for children with autism spectrum disorder in the New York City Department of Education and was honored as the 2012 New York State Adapted Physical Education Teacher of the Year. Dr. Haegele has also been co-director of Camp Abilities Alaska, a one-week developmental sport camp for children with visual impairments, since 2009.

Cathy Houston-Wilson, PhD, is a professor at The College at Brockport in the Department of Kinesiology, Sport Studies and Physical Education. Her areas of expertise are in Adapted Physical Education, Early Childhood Physical Education and Fitness Education. She has authored and co-authored numerous books, books chapters, and articles throughout her thirty-year career in education. Dr. Houston-Wilson received her PhD from Oregon State University in Movement Studies in Disability, her MS from The College at

Brockport–State University of New York in Adapted Physical Education, and her BS from Manhattan College in Physical Education.

Ellen Kowalski, PhD, is an associate professor in the Department of Health Studies, Physical Education, and Human Performance Science at Adelphi University. She teaches in the area of adapted physical education, motor development, motor learning, and rhythms and movement fundamentals in the teacher preparation curriculum.

Lauren J. Lieberman, PhD, is Distinguished Service Professor in the Department of Kinesiology, Sport Studies and Physical Education, The College at Brockport–State University of New York. An acknowledged expert in the physical education of students with visual impairments and deafblindness, she founded in 1996 the Camp Abilities, a sports camp for children who are visually impaired, blind, or deafblind, with eighteen affiliates in other states and seven countries. Dr. Lieberman is the winner of the 2012 Access Award from the American Foundation for the Blind and the 2012 Professional of the Year Award from the Adapted Physical Activity Council of the American Alliance for Health, Physical Education, Recreation and Dance and is on the board of directors of the U.S. Association for Blind Athletes.

Matthew Mescall is currently an Adapted Physical Education and Health teacher at The Maryland School for the Blind. He is a 2011 graduate of New York State College at Brockport, where he was awarded the APAC's (Adapted Physical Activity Council) National Most Outstanding Undergraduate of the Year. For the past six years, Mescall has been a specialist at Camp Abilities Alaska, one-week developmental sports camp for children who are blind or visually impaired, and co-directs Camp Abilities Maryland. Mescall was nominated for the POSB (Principals of Schools for the Blind) 2015 Outstanding Teacher of Students who are blind or visually impaired.

Amaury Samalot-Rivera was born and raised in the island of Puerto Rico. Currently an assistant professor at The College at Brockport–State University of New York in the area of Physical Education Teaching Department since 2013. He taught for ten years in the Elementary and Special Physical Education Department of the University of Puerto Rico at Bayamon, where he was the accreditation coordinator and student teaching coordinator. Samalot-Rivera has a bachelor's degree in secondary physical education from University of Puerto Rico at Mayaguez and a master's and a doctoral degree from The Ohio State University in Adapted Physical Education.

Dr. Garth Tymeson is a full professor in the Department of Exercise and Sport Science at the University of Wisconsin–La Crosse, where he directs and teaches in the graduate and undergraduate adapted physical education teacher preparation programs. He directs the Center on Disability Health and Adapted Physical Activity. Dr. Tymeson has been active in the National Consortium on Physical Education for Individuals with Disabilities. Dr. Tymeson completed his PhD in adapted physical education and special education at Texas Woman's University; MS in adapted physical education at The College of Brockport–State University of New York; a BS in physical education at The College of Cortland–State University of New York; and an Associate of Arts at Hudson Valley Community College in his hometown of Troy, NY.

Linda Webbert, Certified Adapted Physical Educator, is an Adapted Physical Education Resource teacher for Baltimore County Public Schools. Her primary responsibility is to assist physical education teachers in providing appropriate instruction in physical education to students with disabilities. She was the 1999 Maryland Adapted Physical Education Teacher of the Year and has given presentations throughout the United States on teaching and including students with disabilities into educational and recreational programs.